GARDENING WITH C

Nick Romanowski is a biologist and also a commercial
grower of aquatic and water's edge plants, maintaining
one of the world's most diverse wetland collections in his
southern Australian nursery, Dragonfly Aquatics. He is the
author of numerous books and articles on the propagation
and identification of aquatic plants, on wetland creation
and planting, and on aquaculture.

Florida A&M University, Tallahassee
Florida Atlantic University, Boca Raton
Florida Gulf Coast University, Ft. Myers
Florida International University, Miami
Florida State University, Tallahassee
University of Central Florida, Orlando
University of Florida, Gainesville
University of North Florida, Jacksonville
University of South Florida, Tampa
University of West Florida, Pensacola

Darlingtonia californica

GARDENING WITH
CARNIVORES

SARRACENIA PITCHER PLANTS
IN CULTIVATION & IN THE WILD

Nick Romanowski

University Press of Florida

Gainesville/Tallahassee/Tampa/Boca Raton
Pensacola/Orlando/Miami/Jacksonville/Ft. Myers

Copyright 2002 by Nick Romanowski

Published in Sydney, Australia,
by University of New South Wales Press Ltd.

Published simultaneously in the United States
of America by the University Press of Florida.
All North American rights reserved.

07 06 05 04 03 02   6 5 4 3 2 1

ISBN 0-8130-2509-5

Library of Congress cataloging-in-publication
data are available.

The University Press of Florida is the scholarly
publishing agency for the State University System
of Florida, comprising Florida A&M University,
Florida Atlantic University, Florida Gulf Coast
University, Florida International University,
Florida State University, University of Central
Florida, University of Florida, University of
North Florida, University of South Florida, and
University of West Florida.

University Press of Florida
15 Northwest 15th Street
Gainesville, FL 32611-2079
http://www.upf.com

CONTENTS

S. purpurea subsp. *venosa* in winter.

ACKNOWLEDGMENTS

As usual with my books, this one was really started on long before I had ever thought of writing, so I have forgotten the names of many people who have provided plants and information over the decades. To those neglected contacts, I can only apologise for not keeping better records over the years. More recently in the research, photography and writing for this book, I have been helped in many ways by quite a few skilled and knowledgeable people including Ron Abernethy, Peter Anderson, Peter Bloem, Colin Clayton, Fred Howell, Bernadette Lingham, Allen Lowrie and Gordon Ohlenrott, with some constructive editing by Brendan Atkins.

Particular thanks to Roger Spencer at the Melbourne Herbarium and Barry Conn at the Sydney Herbarium for checking drafts of the first part, Robert Gibson for his comments on the manuscript as a whole, and to Barry Meyers-Rice and Don Schnell in the USA who promptly and courteously replied to my barrage of letters and queries during the final stages of writing. However, any errors of fact or interpretation remaining should be blamed on the author!

Thanks also to the many growers and collectors who have shared their experiences with *Sarracenia* in diverse journals. Without these articles (particularly in the *Carnivorous Plant Newsletter*, the *Bulletin of the Australian Carnivorous Plant Society*, and the *Carnivorous Plant Society Journal*) it would have been difficult to write anything like a comprehensive account.

Although all sketches and nearly all of the photography in this book are my own, I am indebted to the people below for allowing me to draw upon their photos of wild plants, and of habitats. Robert Gibson loaned prints of *S.* x *catesbaei* and the same wild plant back-crossed with *S. purpurea*, as well as slides of *S. flava* var. *rubricorpora* with typical *S. flava* in Apalachicola County (Florida), and *S. flava* regrowth in a fire-managed Florida swamp. Stephen Locke provided slides of wild plants of *S. alata*, *S.* x *moorei* and *S. leucophylla* on a residential property, and of Okefenokee Swamp, while Don Schnell loaned a slide of *Exyra* grub damage in *S. leucophylla*.

In the slide of *Sarracenia* pitchers used as cut flowers, the blue pots were made by Robert Mills, and the Jacky lizard vase by Damien Meehan.

S. x courtii

INTRODUCTION

Carnivorous plants are among the most visually fascinating and biologically intriguing of plants, and among these the North American pitchers (*Sarracenia*) stand out with their bold, sculptural shapes, vivid colours and patterns, and easily observed and understood prey capture behaviours. For biologists dealing with recent evolutionary ideas, the entire group is potentially a living showcase of biology in action at many levels. As their hidden lives are increasingly probed it is becoming clear that there is far more to their ecology and genetics than has been imagined.

Although most people regard pitcher plants as an exotic, hothouse novelty, all *Sarracenia* are cold-tolerant garden plants and many can be grown from parts of southern Canada to Florida, across most of the United Kingdom and much of Europe, and through most of non-tropical Australia and New Zealand. Some gardeners (and many collectors) are becoming aware that these striking plants are not just easy to grow outdoors, but will colour up most dramatically in full sunlight, while eating their way through vast numbers of pest insects from wasps to flies, blowflies and ants.

Little of the more recent scientific information on this exciting group has been widely available. This book brings together academic and practical knowledge, blended whenever possible with the aim of adding new dimensions to growing and appreciating *Sarracenia*. A final section looks at the commercial potential of the pitchers as a cash crop, the first time this has been evaluated in detail. Whatever the reader's interests and background, I hope this book will give both pleasure and new insights into a group of plants which is becoming increasingly important to scientists and gardeners, and has a promising future in horticulture and aquaculture as well.

NAMES & PRONUNCIATION

Botanists, growers and many other people familiar with the North American pitcher plants use formal scientific names for them. This is partly because common names can be misleading — although the scientific names often just mean the same thing! For example, Pale Pitcher (referring to the pale flower colour) includes some of the blackest pitchers, while the yellow-flowered Yellow Pitcher includes deep red to purple pitcher forms. But for readability both the publishers and I have chosen to use common names to avoid turning the book into something reading like a monograph.

Scientific names are part of a well-defined system, where the first properly published name for any plant should be used with little or no modification thereafter. As in any legal-type system some exceptions and changes may be made with increasing knowledge of the plants, though these are unlikely to make much difference to the eight to ten *Sarracenia* (pronounced 'SARR-UH-SEE-NEE-UH') species.

The hardest part of a scientific name for most people is pronunciation of this peculiar mix of Latin, Greek, and names of people and places. The pronunciations for scientific names suggested below are used by *Sarracenia* enthusiasts everywhere, regardless of their native accents, and the common names are those which are used throughout this book. Two other *Sarracenia* which are sometimes treated as separate species are treated as subspecies of Sweet Pitcher in this book. These are Canebreak Pitcher (*S. rubra* subsp. *alabamensis*, pronounced 'AL-AH-BAM-EN-SIS'), and Mountain Pitcher (*S. rubra* subsp. *jonesii*, pronounced 'JONES-EE-IY'), these names referring to the USA state and a person respectively.

PALE PITCHER The name *S. alata* refers to the keel (ala) on the front of the pitcher, although this is better developed in some other species. Pronounce this 'AH-LAH-TAH'.

YELLOW PITCHER *S. flava* means 'yellow', referring to flower colour in particular. Pronounce this 'F-LAH-VAH'.

WHITE PITCHER *S. leucophylla* means 'white leaf', and is pronounced 'LL-YOO-KOH-FY-LAH'.

SWEET PITCHER *S. rubra* means 'red' (though there are redder forms in other *Sarracenia* species), and is pronounced 'ROO-BRUH'.

Heliamphora nutans

PURPLE PITCHER *S. purpurea* means 'purple', and is pronounced 'PURR-PEW-REE-UH'.

GREEN PITCHER *S. oreophila* means 'mountain-loving', and is pronounced 'OR-EY-OH-FY-LAH'.

HOODED PITCHER *S. minor* means smallish or relatively insignificant compared to other species, though few forms of this plant are particularly small, and this is pronounced 'MY-NOR'.

PARROT PITCHER *S. psittacina* refers to the parrot-like beak of the pitchers, and is pronounced 'SIT-AH-CHEE-NUH'.

part one

SARRACENIA IN THE WILD

Two very different forms of Sarracenia flava *growing wild in northern Florida.*

HISTORY, HABITAT AND FUNCTION

Among the hundreds of families of flowering plants, only ten are definitely known to include species that can trap animals. All of these grow in nutrient-poor places, where an ability to find alternative sources of substances missing from their soil or water gives them a competitive edge over other plants — often a significant one. Their victims are usually small insects and crustaceans, but these provide a rich source of nitrogen, phosphorus and probably other nutrients as they are broken down by bacteria, fungi or, in many cases, the plant's own juices.

Most of these ten families have only a few carnivorous representatives, but some seem to specialise in an animal trapping lifestyle. These carnivorous groups aren't just minor variations on the same theme, but develop completely different approaches to capturing their prey. This diversity of techniques might suggest that an appetite for flesh is just about all they have in common, yet even a casual glance at their flowers will show how closely related the carnivorous plants of any one family are.

In the Droseraceae, the four carnivorous genera use three distinct types of trap. Sundews (*Drosera*) have an abundance of sticky, stalked glands to which their prey stick, while *Drosophyllum* slaps a different sticky material all over its victims without actually holding on to them (this plant is probably best separated into its own family, the Drosophyllaceae). By contrast, the leaves of the Venus Flytrap (*Dionaea*) actively trap insects, and the similar traps of the Water Wheel Plant (*Aldrovanda*) snap shut on submerged animals that bump into them.

Among the Lentibulariaceae, the three carnivorous genera use distinct techniques. The elongated, root-like, slitted traps of *Genlisea* guide prey to a digestive chamber, while buttery-feeling leaves of *Pinguicula* glue small insects before actively digesting them, and *Utricularia* has numerous tiny bladders which snap shut as they suck in passing victims.

^ A variable wild stand of S. alata *in Alabama.*

^ Hollow-leaved Sea Lavender (S. purpurea subsp. purpurea) *(after an early woodblock print).*

∨ *Heliamphora nutans*

The largest and most spectacular traps are pitchers, most evolved in three unrelated plant families. The Cephalotaceae has just the Albany Pitcher Plant (*Cephalotus*), while the tropical Nepenthaceae has perhaps ninety species all in the one genus *Nepenthes*. Interestingly, recent genetic studies suggest that *Nepenthes* shares a common ancestor with *Drosophyllum*, though probably a very long time ago. The Sarraceniaceae, with three genera — *Heliamphora*, *Darlingtonia* and *Sarracenia* — is more diverse than the other two families, though it probably has only around fifteen species.

Heliamphora grow as groups of apparently simple cups on the high, rain-swept plateaus of tropical South America. The woody tissues of these plants suggest that their tropical home is closer to the original habitats of the family than those of *Sarracenia* (and *Darlingtonia*), which show specialisations for more temperate climates. However, they have probably evolved in their own direction for some time as their distinct chromosome count (42) suggests. Their hood doesn't keep rain out of the pitcher effectively, but its protected spoon tip produces nectar and fragrance. In the largest species (*H. tatei*) this tip shows vividly in bright light and seems very attractive to various types of flies and mosquitoes, while the smaller species seem better at trapping ants and beetles.

On the west coast of the USA, the Cobra Lily (*Darlingtonia californica*) forms extensive colonies in seep bogs. Its relationship to *Sarracenia* is obvious, but the pitchers twist a full half circle as they rise so they face outwards, with a curving keel apparently well adapted for guiding ants and beetles upwards to the mouth. These pitchers are also said to be particularly attractive to flying insects, including butterflies. The trap form is basically similar to that of *S. psittacina*, but with a chromosome count of 30 compared to the 26 of

Sarracenia, the two genera have probably been evolving separately for a long time.

The genus *Sarracenia* has eight to ten species (depending on how the variation in one group is interpreted), all of these occurring in the south-eastern USA where their main range runs from eastern Texas to southern Virginia. However, Purple Pitcher (*S. purpurea*) also extends much further north, with a subspecies extending through Canada as far as British Columbia in the west. The species are discussed in detail in the next section, 'The species'.

EARLY RECORDS

It has not apparently been recorded what Native Americans knew or thought about pitcher plants, but to the early European explorers in North America they must have been a strange and alien sight. Yet the first record of a pitcher plant doesn't appear until 1576, an illustration of Hooded Pitcher in *Nova Stirpium Adversaria* by de l'Obel (latinised as Lobelius), which was probably collected in Florida by Spaniards. In 1601, a handsome plate of the northern variant of *S. purpurea* was published in *Rariorum Plantarum Historiam* by de l'Ecluse (Clusius).

This also represented the first attempt to decide on the relationship of pitcher plants to the rest of the plant kingdom. Lacking anything but a dried specimen, Clusius tentatively placed it with the Sea Lavenders (as *Limonium peregrinum*) based on its thickened leaves. Although he was plainly aware that living material might show very different relationships, this early name was resurrected in 1672 as Hollow-leaved Lavender in Josselyn's *New England Rarities*. Clusius' plate had also reappeared around 1630 in an English botanical magazine, as a result of which living plants were brought into England in 1637, and listed as being in cultivation by the botanist John Tradescant in 1640.

The present name *Sarracenia* was published in 1700 by Tournefort, after a physician and part-time botanist at the Court of Quebec, Michel Sarrazin de l'Etang. Other species began to appear under this genus as they were described, though it is just as well that some of the early names, published before Linnaeus established the basis of contemporary scientific nomenclature, have disappeared: Catesby's 1731 version of Yellow Pitcher as *Sarracenia foliis longioribus et angustioribus* will certainly not be missed!

Catesby also made one of the earliest suggestions on the function of the pitcher leaves, thinking that they might be a refuge for insects from predatory species such as frogs and other animals. Other authors suggested the design was altruistic, providing water for thirsty birds! It was Charles Darwin who first seems to have guessed their true purpose in 1875, though it was another twelve years before Dr Joseph H. Mellichamp demonstrated digestion and absorption of venison pieces by pitchers.

PITCHER PLANT HABITATS

In the southern parts of their range, pitcher plants are generally found growing in seasonally boggy, sandy soils that have often been left as sea levels fall. In swampy areas, these are usually peaty from the slow breakdown of organic matter in waterlogged conditions, and can be fairly acidic (around pH 5). It has often been assumed that larger wetlands of this kind have developed over hundreds of thousands of years, but more recent studies suggest that even the sprawling Okefenokee Swamp (mostly in Georgia, but extending just over the border into Florida) is probably only between 5000 and 8000 years old, the result of sluggish rivers banking up over coastal lowlands as sea levels rose after the last ice age.

S. minor in Okefenokee Swamp.

These wetlands include a diverse array of plants, but healthy *Sarracenia* communities are found only in the most open areas. In the past, such areas were kept open by summer lightning fires, or winter fires set by Native Americans to maintain a rich patchwork of game and forage plots. The pitcher plants grow and reproduce best where fire has cleared competing plants, and are frequently associated with other fire-adapted species. Of these, the tall and widespread Wiregrass (*Aristida stricta*) burns readily even when green, resprouting days after a burn, and will produce its seed only after a summer fire.

The climate in the south-east is warm temperate overall, with warm to hot summers and relatively light frosts. Humidity generally remains high as rain falls throughout the year, though more southerly areas tend to be drier during winter. In summer, rain is often associated with the frequent lightning storms which once would have started many natural fires. Although pitcher plant wetlands are often fed by runoff from rain, the water level in sandier soils rises and falls with the underground water table. This can drop considerably during prolonged drought periods, so the plants have to be fairly drought tolerant.

Snow is rare and sparse when it falls, but light frosts are not uncommon, particularly inland. Even in our present mild interglacial period, freezes to −12°C (10°F) have lasted days in Florida, icing over saltwater bays. It is not surprising that all pitcher species are far more cold tolerant than most growers would suspect, as these areas must have been colder still at the peak of the previous ice age!

To the south, *Sarracenia* species diversity drops off rapidly on the Florida peninsula, as the species have had little chance to move into this low and relatively recently raised land. Here, Sweet Pitcher is found only in the far north-west of the State (the 'Panhandle'), Parrot Pitcher just makes it

into the northern part, Yellow Pitcher a little further south, and Hooded Pitcher (which is perhaps more tolerant of drier winters) a fair way down the neck to Okeechobee County.

Further north, the diversity of pitcher plants falls away less rapidly. Of the species found in the east, Parrot Pitcher just reaches into South Carolina, Hooded Pitcher just into North Carolina, and Yellow and Sweet Pitchers to southern Virginia. These plants are found in increasingly rich soils, often in sphagnum bogs where they may grow in permanently wet places. Only Purple Pitcher extends beyond Virginia, reaching far across Canada. To the west, only Pale Pitcher shows any significant variation, with some of the blackest-coloured variants in eastern Texas.

PLANTS AND THEIR PITCHERS

Sarracenia grow from underground rhizomes, thick and fleshy stems that can sometimes surface and even float in the two most aquatic species, Parrot Pitcher and Purple Pitcher. New growing points appear along the rhizome, which may branch repeatedly. Looked at from above each growing point, the pitchers generally face inwards towards the centre.

As in many other wetland plants, this growth habit makes it difficult to work out how long any single plant has lived. It is possible that some very uniform-looking stands of pitcher plants in the wild are just a few, long-lived and widely spread individuals. It is even possible that some are a single clone, as I have been able to demonstrate for a self-sterile clone of an Australian sedge occupying most of an 11-hectare (27-acre) wetland. Such plants are likely to be hundreds of years old at the least — but the lifespan of wild *Sarracenia* is still unknown.

Unlike animals, carnivorous plants don't obtain their energy needs from the small animals they trap — these are just a source of nutrients (particularly nitrogen and phosphorus) which in turn are building blocks for more complex chemicals in the plant. The energy source for almost all flowering plants including carnivorous ones is sunlight. This light energy is collected by a pigment called chlorophyll (the green colour in most types of leaves) during photosynthesis, and is used to combine carbon dioxide and water into simple, energy-storing compounds which are the starting point for more complex reactions.

than Green Pitcher, with both pitchers and flowers remaining green or yellow.

As well as producing all of the plant's energy needs through photosynthesis, the leaves form a pitcher by remaining joined along their front edge, where other leaves would separate and open out. This joined edge may be quite wide, and is called an ala or wing. Pitchers would probably be a fairly effective trap even as a plain vertical tube, as long as they are large enough to let insects in, yet not so large that flying insects would have room to fly out.

S. leucophylla *showing the insect-directing hairs of Zone 1, and the beginning of the smooth, waxy Zone 2.*

Most photosynthesis happens in the leaves, which in *Sarracenia* are the pitchers. However, in White Pitcher, Parrot Pitcher and Hooded Pitcher, some parts of the leaves don't have any chlorophyll in them and so they look white. The other colours seen in the various *Sarracenia* are separate pigments to the green chlorophyll, so even a deep-red or blackish-looking pitcher will probably photosynthesise just as well as an all-green pitcher of the same species. Red *Sarracenia* pigments are known as anthocyanins, but mutant forms lacking any red pigmentation are known in all species other

To increase effectiveness in trapping, different zones of the upright species are modified to be attractive to insects, and to make dropping in as easy as falling off a log. The pitcher forms in Purple Pitcher and Parrot Pitcher are somewhat different, and these are discussed in the 'The species'. Zone 1 is the hood of the pitcher, which helps to shed rain in most species, and is lined with inward pointing hairs that encourage insect movement down towards the next zone. The inside of the hood is often brightly coloured or marked as well, presumably to attract insects, and may have

further patterning which is only visible to insects with ultraviolet vision. This is not mimicry as has sometimes been suggested, but advertising!

Zone 2 is around the mouth of the pitcher and the inside neck supporting the hood. The surface is usually smooth and sometimes slick with nectar, which is produced as an added attractant by small glands here and on the lip (also called a nectar roll). Zone 2 may extend down into the neck for a small distance, and offers little grip for insect feet. In Yellow Pitcher at least, the nectar contains a narcotic (coniine) which paralyses potential prey. This species also becomes more attractive to blowflies as it fills, because of the increasing smell of decaying bodies inside. The same principle is used in some human-made flytraps.

Zone 3 is waxy and completely smooth, and may also secrete 'digestive' fluids. It offers virtually no resistance for the downward slide into Zone 4, where downward pointing hairs direct prey into the digestive area. Digestion in Zone 4 is accelerated by enzymes and acids in some *Sarracenia*, though not all, and by various fungi and bacteria which are adapted to life in the chemical brew at the bottom. The main nutrients gained from the prey are nitrogen and phosphorus in useable forms, and these are stored in the plant tissues in greater quantities if available. Calcium, magnesium and potassium levels in pitcher plant tissues remain much the same whether the plants collect any prey or not, which suggests they can obtain enough of these nutrients from even the poorest soil or water.

As the pitcher fills with prey, the chitinous shells of insects tend to collapse downwards under their own weight, though eventually the pitcher may fill to the point that late arrivals can walk out over the lip. The numbers of insects that are trapped can be very large — a single big trap of Yellow Pitcher may contain the remains of around a thousand flies and wasps. Occasional larger victims including frogs have also been recorded, perhaps slipping in while in pursuit of trapped insects.

Other would-be victims have other ways out, particularly spiders, which can drop in to remove insects and escape along the thread of silk they leave spun out behind them. Larger-jawed insects can simply chew their way through the side of the pitcher, while some flies drop eggs into the pitcher so their larvae can feed on the accumulating bodies until ready to pupate and fly out.

New pitchers appear on plants in spring, in some species being replaced fairly continuously through the whole growing season. In others they come in two growth flushes — spring and autumn. The lifespan of each pitcher also varies between species, from several weeks to approximately two months. Autumn pitchers are often the most brightly coloured, possibly affected by falling temperatures, but this is also possibly related to drier conditions or different light conditions, as can be seen in many unrelated wetland plant families and genera.

In winter, some pitcher species (particularly the Yellow Pitcher and Green Pitcher) produce a different kind of leaf called a phyllode (plural: phyllodia), which is long and flattened. The phyllodia continue photosynthesis during the winter months even after the pitchers have shrivelled. For this reason, if they are cut off

< Sectioned S. rubra *subsp.* gulfensis *showing Zones 2, 3 and 4.*

˅ Winter phyllodia of S. flava.

> Flowers of S. flava, *appearing well before the pitchers.*

along with the dead pitchers, spring growth may not be as vigorous as in undamaged plants. In cultivated plants in mild climates, some phyllodia may form a small pitcher towards their tip.

FLOWERING AND POLLINATION

Sarracenia flowers usually have five petals, and are designed to encourage cross-pollination by other flowers. Mutants with greater numbers of petals are known, and though these may be attractive they are usually sterile. All flowers open facing downwards, held above the pitchers on stems which may reach 70 centimetres (over 2 feet) or more in some species, around a metre (3 feet) in some hybrids. The flowering season for *Sarracenia* spreads from early spring to early summer over its wide range. Many produce blooms before their pitchers open, presumably an adaptation that avoids catching potential pollinators, but this varies between species, populations and climates.

Where the stem joins the flower, there are three slightly fleshy, petal-like bracts, with a ring of five sepals next. Below the

sepals is the swollen ovary, which must be fertilised to produce seed. Stamens encircle the base of the ovary, each one tipped with pollen-producing anthers. The ovary narrows to a stalk (the style), and this opens out at its end into a five-cornered, upside-down parasol — the style umbrella (or disc). On the inside of each of the five tips of the umbrella is a stigma (plural: stigmata), where pollen must be brushed if the flower is to be fertilised. Five petals hang like drapes from the base of the ovary.

Sarracenia is the only genus in its family with nectar glands in the flower, which have been described as a 'more luxuriant' version of the 14-celled nectar glands found in Zone 2 of the pitchers. The nectar is produced near the base of the petals by the glands, which are in the skin of the ovary. This acts as bait that guides insects (particularly bees) through the flower in the right sequence for cross-pollination by other plants. Fragrance may also be an

important attractant in some species, although this is often noticeable only on newly opened blooms.

Most *Sarracenia* flowers are colourful and can be seen from a distance. Although red pigments are often the most obvious, yellow and sometimes blue pigments are also often present and may be visible to pollinators, even if not to the human eye. Insects tend to land near the base of a petal, drawn by the nectar fragrance. From here, they push through the spaces between the petals, where these meet over the five stigmas on the points of the umbrella. As an insect pushes in, pollen collected from earlier visits to other flowers will be scraped off by the petals, falling onto and around the stigmata.

Having delivered its pollen cargo, the insect now climbs to the ovary to gather nectar, and as it scrambles around is dusted with fresh pollen from the stamens, which it will carry to the next flower it visits. The insect may also pick up fresh pollen where it rains down to the upward-curved floor of the umbrella. To leave the flower, the insect just has to push any one of the five loosely attached petals outwards, which is easiest to do between the spokes at the lower lip of the umbrella. This easy exit reduces the chance of pollination in the plant with its own pollen from insects contacting any of the higher stigmata a second time.

Once the flower is pollinated, the petals fall off — they will do so in any case after about two weeks, even if the flower is not pollinated. The bracts, sepals, ovary and style umbrella remain, tilting to a more horizontal position as seed begins to develop in the ovary. This has the effect of preventing

falling seed from being caught in the umbrella later. The smaller flowers of the smaller species generally tilt less than those of large ones as they mature, presumably because these are less likely to trap their own seed.

SEEDS AND GERMINATION

After fertilisation, the ovary swells and matures to become a seed capsule, browning off and splitting along its five seams to release the seed around early autumn. In most species the capsule shrivels and dries from the tip, except in White Pitcher where it shrivels from the base. This may be an adaptation to minimise seed capture by the style umbrella.

The seeds are small, up to about 2 mm long (slightly under 0.1 inch). Depending on the species, it may take between a thousand and two thousand dry seeds to make up a gram (0.03 ounces). Seed production per capsule varies between species, from as few as a hundred seeds in smaller capsules of Hooded Pitcher, to about a thousand in a Yellow Pitcher capsule.

The seeds are pale brown to grey-brown or even pinkish, and rough surfaced. As they are very hydrophobic, it can take weeks for them to absorb enough water for germination. This is presumably an adaptation to spreading by floating in sluggish streams or the still waters of enclosed wetlands. Unlike some types of wetland seed, they don't tangle readily into fur or even the finest down feathers (an efficient way for plant species to travel between wetlands). This could explain the relatively limited distribution of most species and many forms.

A cool to cold winter period is essential for good seed germination — usually a minimum of six to eight weeks in moist to wet conditions at temperatures often at or below about 5°C (41°F). In wild populations, seed germination (recruitment) is best by far in open areas with abundant

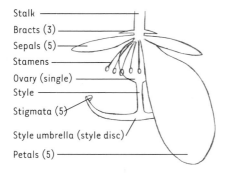

Stalk
Bracts (3)
Sepals (5)
Stamens
Ovary (single)
Style
Stigmata (5)
Style umbrella (style disc)
Petals (5)

Stylised cross-section of a Sarracenia flower, with petals removed to show internal parts.

light, usually after fires when shade from competing plants has been reduced considerably, and nutrients in the ash promote growth. In cultivation, seedlings usually reach flowering size in five to eight years. Some growers claim to achieve this in two years for some hybrids, but this result would be obtained only under totally controlled conditions, and the resulting plants often adapt poorly to outside planting. Figures from wild populations are not available, but it is likely that growth in these is often slower.

HYBRIDISATION AND EVOLUTION

All *Sarracenia* are fully cross-fertile, as are their hybrid offspring. Despite the often-different flowering times of different species where these are found together in the wild, there are almost invariably some hybrids to be found. Hybridisation may be reduced by selectivity in some pollinators such as bees, which tend to 'work' one kind of flower at a time, but the similarity of many pitcher plant flowers means that occasional crosses are inevitable.

Flowers from two different hybrid plants, with the petals removed on the bloom at left to show underlying structure.

It has been suggested that all *Sarracenia* hybrids, not just crosses between different trap types, are both uncommon and at a selective disadvantage compared to their parent species. This idea is largely based on the clumsy and ineffective traps of some Purple Pitcher and Parrot Pitcher hybrids, particularly when crossed with upright trap types. Even some of these are surprisingly effective at looking after themselves, as the great size and obvious good health of many wild *S. x catesbaei* (Yellow Pitcher *S. flava* crossed with Purple Pitcher *S. purpurea*) show. And it is interesting to note that Parrot Pitcher — which has such a different design of trap from any other species that its hybrids are particularly inefficient at trapping prey — is usually the last to flower, so natural hybrids of this species are uncommon.

The argument that other hybrids are also rare does not appear to be based on good evidence, as can be verified by reading any detailed, older account of natural stands. With only one out of forty original *Sarracenia* habitats remaining these days, it is not surprising that contemporary botanists are seeing less hybridisation in the field — the majority of the best sites for observing natural hybridisation must certainly be gone. Yet even now, surprisingly variable natural populations can still be found.

Perhaps the greatest handicap to identifying hybrid elements is the readiness of hybrids to backcross to their parents (known as introgression). Second generation introgressed hybrids are often much like their parent species at first glance, and only close inspection will show that some of their characters may be taken from another species. Furthermore, if either of the parent species has gone locally extinct, the hybrids left will tend to keep introgressing towards the surviving parent species, and can easily be misinterpreted as a 'pure' but variable stand of a single species.

An apparent example of this is a stand of Pale Pitcher in Stone County, Mississippi, which has numerous and diverse plants including large pubescent green ones, types with wavy red lids, heavily veined plants and all-red plants including some that are almost black on the outside. Some even have hoods reminiscent of Hooded Pitcher but without any trace of the white windows (also called fenestrations or areolae) of that species. It is hard to imagine that such variability could occur in a single population without some hybrid elements being present.

Hybridisation doesn't just occur between pitcher species, but also between distinct variants (or morphs) of a single species. The diverse pattern and colour morphs of Yellow Pitcher are an excellent example of this. Some such as variety *rugelii* occur mainly in large, pure stands; others may be found in single variety stands or mixed with other *Sarracenia*, and frequent hybrids among them. Polymorphism often suggests active evolution, and as the various morphs don't appear to be absorbed or averaged out through hybridisation, there must be strong selective advantages

< S. x catesbaei x S. purpurea, *detail of a plant growing at the base of a larger parent plant* S. catesbaei *(Drosera fili-formis var.* tracyi *in foreground).*

∨ S. x catesbaei *in north-western Florida, a large plant with smaller back-crosses to* S. pur-purea *in foreground, growing with Drosera capillaris and D. fili-formis var.* tracyi.

for each type to tend to revert back towards one or the other parent.

This situation is comparable to that in interspecies hybrid swarms, where gene flow is obviously happening between distinct species. Although both parent morphs or species will tend to maintain their own distinctive anatomy, the possibility of new and useful genes being captured and eventually integrated from another morph or species is intriguing.

Combined with other specialisations such as carnivory, introgression makes *Sarracenia* potentially one of the most exciting and plastic, yet readily accessible and manipulated, plant groups available for research both in laboratories and the wild. Their evolutionary interest may extend even further than the hybridisation aspects discussed briefly here, because the northern subspecies of Purple Pitcher is perhaps an example of rapid geographic expansion and speciation.

INSECT ASSOCIATES

Like all wild plants, *Sarracenia* have many insects associated with or feeding on them. Best known and often most visible in their effects are *Exyra* moths, whose small, purple-and-white striped larvae feed and pupate within the pitchers. There are three species of these: *E. rolandiana* (synonym *E. fax*) only in the northern subspecies of Purple Pitcher; *E. ridingsii* in Yellow Pitcher only; and *E. semicrocea* feeding on all species except in the northern range.

Usually the female lays only a single orange egg per pitcher. The larva feeds on the inside layer of the pitcher until the top is so weakened that it collapses. This prevents access by other moths, although the larva may also close off the top of the pitcher with a silken web at an earlier stage, presumably for the same purpose. The larva may change pitchers several times, damaging a number of them on the same plant, and will also damage flowers and eat seeds. A study of *E. semicrocea* in Hooded Pitcher in Florida found that it had rendered two-thirds of the leaves non-functional, and there were young larvae in over one-fifth of the remaining intact pitchers.

Before pupating, the larva cuts two holes in the lower part of its pitcher, the lower one for drainage and the upper one to escape through once it has emerged as a jawless moth. The moths are also highly adapted to life in and around pitchers, hiding head-up inside these without slipping, and even retreating deeper if disturbed or rapidly flying to another pitcher. During winter, they often hide in shrivelled pitchers from the previous season, so their numbers may be controlled by regular winter burns. However, some individual moths overwinter on the ground outside the pitchers, so they are less vulnerable to fire at this time.

Other larvae feeding on pitcher plants include *Endothenia habesana*, which seems to specialise in flowers and seeds. The *Sarracenia* root-borer (*Papaipema appasionata*) is a substantial grub to around 5 centimetres (2 inches) long, causing extensive damage while hidden within the rhizome. The only obvious signs of its presence are the mounds of orange droppings it excretes near the tip of the rhizome, where new pitchers appear.

Other insects are less destructive on the plants, though they may still prevent pitchers from trapping effectively, or rob them of significant amounts of nutrient. The grass-cutting wasp *Isodontia mexicana* alternates plugs of grass inside a pitcher with paralysed crickets, each one with a single egg laid within so its larvae can feed on fresh food. Several flies (including *Sarcophaga sarraceniae* and *Neosciara macfarlaei*) also lay eggs in pitchers so their maggots can feed on the decaying matter within the pitcher, *Neosciara* larvae closing off the pitcher with a fine and frothy web. The larvae of another Sarcophagid fly were found to consume around half of the insect prey captured, but it is likely that their wastes also provided nutrients for the plants.

CONSERVATION

Throughout the world, wetlands are being destroyed at an incredible rate. The most significant losses are through drainage, agricultural and residential runoff, and inappropriate management, leading to the disappearance of whole ecological communities under weeds, agriculture and forestry. As much of their range lies in some of the most intensely used and populated parts of the USA, *Sarracenia* communities are among the hardest hit of all wetland plants. It has been estimated that as few as 2.5 per cent of their habitats remain in anything like healthy condition, and most of the larger stands of the past are gone.

The future for the remaining populations is not promising without considerable human

∧ S. leucophylla pitcher with top collapsed after Exyra larva damage.

> A wild stand of S. leucophylla (among Longleaf Pine, Pinus palustris) left to grow on private land by owners who value these spectacular plants.

intervention, particularly to manage weeds and taller, woody plants which move into areas where water tables have been lowered through drainage. Canebreak Pitcher, Green Pitcher and Mountain Pitcher are all reduced to a few small populations or even isolated plants in places, but many populations of less endangered species have also been reduced to a few odd plants barely surviving along the drainage ditches used to lower the water tables in their formerly wet savannahs.

Ideally, wetlands should be conserved as adequately sized blocks with substantial buffer zones around them to minimise disturbance of all kinds. This is no longer possible in many areas where privately owned lands overlap parts of the watershed, so neighbouring drainage schemes can affect the hydrology (water flows and retention) of the protected place. The management of wetlands is also affected by the increasing land uses around reserved areas. Fire is an important tool in restoring some types of degraded wetlands, but is feared by people who aren't aware of how easily it can be controlled in the appropriate season.

Grazing by cattle may keep competing weeds down in a *Sarracenia* swamp, as they avoid eating the pitchers, perhaps because of the smell of decaying insects within, or the bitter alkaloids in the leaves. However, cattle droppings also bring in a diversity of highly competitive weed seeds which create further problems and are difficult to eradicate. Cattle also cause long-term harm by compacting and eroding soils under their hooves, crushing seedlings, and causing the

gradual build-up of nutrients in the soil.

Conservation bodies such as The Nature Conservancy are increasingly encouraging landowners to understand and appreciate wetlands, but the education needed to achieve this takes time and older landowners are often resistant to new ideas. Other groups including the Atlanta Botanical Garden are successfully experimenting with the restoration of degraded wetland habitats, first by restoring natural hydrology through closing off drains, then by burning and slashing to clear competing vegetation.

Their results suggest that winter fires have the most impact on restoring severely overgrown areas, preventing seed formation by weedy species, and also allowing faster nutrient leaching. This keeps soil nutrient levels low and encourages pitcher plant growth, rather than competing plants. For some *Sarracenia*, it has been shown that pitcher regrowth is more generous in recently burned plots, especially for the small Parrot Pitcher which is easily shaded. Successful establishment of seedlings is also more likely after fire, and is directly related to how much seed was set in the previous flowering season.

Winter burns reduce the numbers of destructive insect larvae, especially *Exyra*

moth larvae which often overwinter in dead pitchers from the previous season. By contrast, summer burns allow a more natural diversity of plants adapted to natural fires to build up, and even annual summer burns don't set pitcher plants back as much as they do their competitors. There is some evidence that small populations of several montane pitchers may survive under dense overgrowth for decades, and can recover rapidly after fire has cleared competing plants.

Some of the remaining stands of White Pitcher are presently being harvested for floristry, which is justified by landowners and lessees as making economic gains from such areas without having to

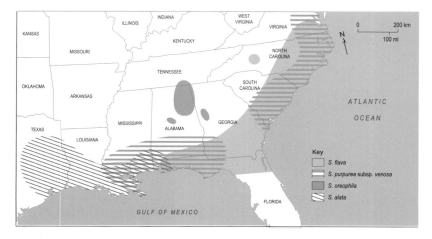

Approximate original range of four Sarracenia *species in south-eastern USA.*

A slow winter burn removes old pitchers of S. flava, leaving the phyllodia mostly unharmed.

Vigorous regrowth of S. flava in Florida, after burning off surrounding saplings.

entire populations by their illegal harvests. Yet it is collectors who are the ultimate cause of this damage. Anyone who buys any of these endangered plants without full documentation as to their source is effectively employing poachers to destroy the last wild stands.

drain them. Whether this is sustainable in the long term remains to be seen, especially as environmental issues become increasingly important and restrictions on such trade are likely to increase with time.

Plants are still being torn from the wild for sale; considering the diversity of quality seed-grown species and hybrids available, this is ecological insanity. Limited amounts of seed or pollen (see 'Cut pitcher production') could probably be harvested under well-regulated permit systems. However, the rarer montane species (Green, Canebreak and Mountain pitchers) are all protected.

These remain particularly endangered because of poachers, who have destroyed

Approximate original range of the remaining four Sarracenia species.

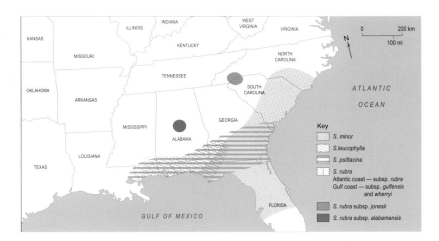

THE SPECIES

Ten major taxa of *Sarracenia* are separated in this section, three of which are so closely related that they are usually regarded as diverse subspecies of Sweet Pitcher. However, a good case could be made for treating Canebreak Pitcher and Mountain Pitcher as separate species.

Several terms used repeatedly in this section can't be avoided for *Sarracenia*. Although it isn't possible to define any of these terms perfectly or to everyone's satisfaction, anyone who has grown or studied the wild plants described will soon have a clear idea of the differences between them.

Subspecies — a markedly distinct population of a species (usually in a different area to other subspecies) which shows consistent physical or genetic differences to

other populations, the significant differences appearing even in cultivated plants. If a subspecies remains sufficiently isolated, it may eventually become different enough to be recognised as a species. Subspecies is sometimes abbreviated to subsp. in this book.

Variety — a relatively minor but consistently different population of plants to others of the same species or subspecies, but not so different that it could ever be mistaken for a wholly different plant. This term is often abbreviated to var.

Form — a minor variation, mutation or even sometimes a sport (with a mutating shoot, bud or flower) which appears among normal populations in some places. Forms are often easily recognisable as

across northern Florida and southern Georgia, along the Atlantic coastal plain to southern Virginia, where it has now largely disappeared.

DESCRIPTION This is the largest and the most widely distributed southern pitcher species. Most forms reach a much greater size (though not necessarily height) than other pitchers, often between 50 centimetres (20 inches) and 90 centimetres (3 feet), exceptionally to over 110 centimetres (44 inches) in cultivation. These are flared at the mouth, with a distinct spout. The large hoods are slightly upturned but relatively flat, and come to a pointed tip, with their rear lobes sometimes being so broad that they overlap behind the pitcher.

The wing (ala) along the front edge of the tube has a nectar trail for attracting ground insects (including beetles) upwards, but much of the prey appears to be flying insects, particularly flies, wasps and some moths. The nectar includes a paralysing agent called coniine which takes effect quickly, making insects clumsy and increasing their chance of a fall. Early victims drown in the digestive juices at the bottom of the pitcher, but these traps are so effective that by the end of the season they may fill almost to the brim, and even collapse under the weight of the insects within them.

The pitchers in many varieties are a bright golden-green, particularly in spring and summer, but some forms continue to produce new growth into the autumn. Frost kills old pitchers, though these may already have shrivelled by mid-autumn even in mild areas. Flattened winter leaves, the phyllodia, are formed as the pitchers collapse or even earlier during late summer, and may last through the winter in good condition. The phyllode is usually described as straight, but it often curves at the tip, sometimes so much so that its end forms a backwards curving sickle shape which may almost reach the ground.

S. purpurea *subsp.* venosa

something a little different from their neighbouring plants — for example, they may have no red pigment, while their siblings all around do.

The order in which species appear below is not alphabetical, but is largely based on natural relationships. This should make it easier to compare similarities and differences.

YELLOW PITCHER S. FLAVA

OTHER COMMON NAMES Yellow Trumpet or Lily.
SYNONYMS S. *fildesii* and S. *gronovii*, and also varieties *atrosanguinea* and *erythropus*.
RANGE From south-eastern Alabama, where it overlaps in a small area with Pale Pitcher,

The yellow flowers are the largest in the genus — up to around 10 centimetres (4 inches) across. They are distinctly fragrant, with a rather musty or feline smell, and appear as early as late winter in the southern parts of the species range, but not until late spring in northern areas. *S. flava* is usually found in seasonally waterlogged places that often dry out as water tables fall during summer. It also grows in more permanently moist or wet situations, such as along slow-moving streams.

VARIETIES Note that there are hybrid plants between these varieties both in nature and in cultivation to which it is not always possible to assign a definite name. Particularly fine, indeterminate clones in cultivation should be registered with a cultivar name, as described in 'Hybrids and hybridising'.

Variety *atropurpurea*: the hood and the outside of the pitcher are deep red, the inside pale tan. It is mostly found on the Atlantic coastal plain, but sometimes in the Florida panhandle as well. In cultivation, these plants will often temporarily lose their rich, red colour if they are divided, moved to new conditions or disturbed in any other way. Plants described as 'Burgundy' in England are probably a colour variant of this formally described variety.

Variety *cuprea*: plants with the upper hood and upper part of the tube a glossy, coppery or rusty colour, often veined as well. It is widespread on the south-eastern coastal plain especially in the Carolinas, and rare in north-western Florida.

Variety *flava*: green plants with variable veining radiating from the deep-red or purple pitcher throat onto the hood and upper part of the pitcher. These plants are known only from the Atlantic coastal plain.

Variety *maxima*: these are all-green plants with a touch of red at the pitcher base, found on both the Atlantic coastal plain and in north-western Florida. They

∧ S. flava *var.* cuprea

> S. flava *var.* rubricorpora

∨ S. alata — *a veined form.*

are quite distinct from the cultivar known as 'Maxima' in England (possibly a hybrid) which is lightly veined, and grey-tinted in the phyllodia and lower part of the pitchers.

Variety *ornata*: the throat in these pitchers is deep red to purple, and extensive networks of veins radiate out from here onto the hood and the tube. Cultivars known as 'heavily-veined' mostly belong here (though some are obviously of hybrid origin), and many of these will flower well, even towards the subtropics, without special treatment. Found in both the Carolinas and north-western Florida.

Variety *rubricor-pora*: the external tube of these plants is dark red, the inside yellow-ish-buff, the hood yellow-green with prominent veins. Found only in north-western Florida.

Variety *rugelii*: pitchers of this variety are wider than those of other varieties with a larger lid, and a deep-red to purple patch in the pitcher throat. This is the dominant variety in southern Georgia, and is also found in

north-western Florida, often forming extensive, yellow-green stands which are a spectacular sight.

YELLOW PITCHER CULTIVARS 'Maxima' has already been described as different from the botanical variety of that name. 'Claret' is of unknown ancestry, a reddish plant with darker red veins. The most distinctive of the named cultivars (possibly lost from cultivation) is 'Marston Dwarf', a heavily-veined plant that reaches only 30 centimetres (12 inches) in height.

PALE PITCHER *S. ALATA*

OTHER COMMON NAMES Flycatcher or Buttercup.

SYNONYMS *S. crispata*, *S. gronovii* var. *alata*, *S. intermedia*, *S. sledgei*.

RANGE The westernmost pitcher plant, growing from eastern Texas, across southern Louisiana, Alabama, and barely into the westernmost part of the Florida panhandle.

DESCRIPTION Pale Pitcher is named for its pale yellow flowers, which may look creamy from a distance in some forms. In Mississippi the petals are yellow enough that they give rise to the name buttercup, looking like shavings of butter overflowing a cup. These have a musty fragrance similar to that of *S. flava* but weaker, and appear from early to middle spring. The species name is from its prominent ala, or wing.

Plants are very variable especially around Alabama, perhaps as a result of hybrid introgression, as this species overlaps with most other southern species and seems particularly able to cross with them. Typical plants are green with red veins, and are often pubescent, with the pitchers reaching around 75 centimetres (30 inches). They are superficially similar to *S. flava*, but the hoods are less flared and are set closer to the mouth; the neck which supports them is much wider, and the mouth is much narrower with no spout.

Other variants include shorter, stockier

pitcher types from north of Mobile, Alabama; types with the inside of the pitcher and hood a deep red approaching black (in cultivation, these are called 'Red Throat' or 'Red Lid'); scalloped hoods; deep red tubes which may approach black as they age (in cultivation called 'Nigra Purpurea'); and even forms with a hood reminiscent of Hooded Pitcher, but with no white fenestrations. The darkest variations are increasingly found towards the Texas end of their range.

This species seems to be found in drier habitats than many other species, at least in the Gulf coast area, though it is also often associated with wet-soil loving species including Parrot, Purple and White pitchers. *S. alata* has been shown to invest more energy in pitchers after fire has reduced competing vegetation, and to store more energy in the rhizomes as competing plants re-establish. This is probably true for other pitcher plant species as well. It can be found on clay soils, on gentle slopes that are wet in spring but dry during summer, and is not uncommonly found as single, isolated plants, which may suggest that the seed is not distributed by water alone. Phyllodia are sometimes produced in dry or exceptionally cold situations.

GREEN PITCHER *S. OREOPHILA*

OTHER COMMON NAMES Flycatcher.
RANGE Mostly patchily distributed in north-eastern Alabama, with three populations in north-east Georgia and south-west North Carolina, and extinct in Tennessee. Around 35 populations survive today.
DESCRIPTION Green Pitcher is closely related to Yellow Pitcher and was only recognised as a separate species in 1933. Indeed, some populations might be difficult to separate if not for their distinct geographic ranges. The ecology of the two species is also different — apparent optimal habitats for this

^ S. oreophila —
a veined form in flower.

> S. leucophylla

species include open, grassy seep slopes which dry out thoroughly by mid-summer, when the pitchers wither and are replaced by phyllodia. Other populations are found near streams, in places which may be seasonally flooded, growing in clay, sand or peatier soils.

The plants are very cold tolerant as they come from relatively high altitudes. Their phyllodia are usually more curved than in the Yellow Pitcher, tilted backwards and often touching the ground, and the pitchers usually have a relatively wider and more rounded opening. The hood is more rounded, somewhat incurved and without a pronounced tip. In the wild, Green Pitcher is said to be the most inefficient insect catcher of all the southern species.

The flowers are pleasantly fragrant

though with some of the mustiness noticeable in Yellow Pitcher. They are a pale greenish-yellow, and reach around 5 centimetres (2 inches) across, appearing from around mid-spring to early summer depending on climate. Young pitchers often show red veining that may disappear as they mature, becoming a very pale green. Some forms retain the veins, particularly Sand Mountain (Alabama) variants, which are often strongly patterned over pale hoods, and even more heavily veined below. The cultivar 'Don Schnell' is perhaps the best coloured of these selections, but is apparently lost to cultivation.

This species is endangered in the wild, where management issues have yet to be fully resolved. Attempts at transplanting and re-establishment have not been notably successful to date. Genetic studies of 14 of the 35 known remaining populations suggest that diversity is low, as

is common in restricted species, and this is particularly so in the smaller populations. Low genetic diversity may also be a problem for recovery programs, if additional planting or pollinating material is not sourced from elsewhere as well.

Even in ideal conditions in cultivation, the plants usually lose their pitchers by around mid-summer, followed sometimes by an early autumn crop of large and strongly veined pitchers which are not long-lasting. The plants divide readily with a high establishment rate. Natural hybrids aren't recorded for this species because of its isolated range, although it does occur with Sweet Pitcher near Birmingham, Alabama. Although seedlings of the species can be difficult to raise, hybrids with other species often show exceptional vigour, as well as large size and good colour.

WHITE PITCHER S. LEUCOPHYLLA

OTHER COMMON NAMES White Trumpet, White-topped Pitcher.

SYNONYMS *S. drummondii, S. gronovii* var. *drummondii, S. laciniata, S. mexicana.* White Pitcher was also originally included with Hooded Pitcher under the name *S. lacunosa*, as material of these two species was described as a single species.

RANGE From the south-eastern corner of Mississippi across southern Alabama, much of the Florida panhandle, and into south-western Georgia.

DESCRIPTION White Pitcher is perhaps the most striking of all the *Sarracenia* species, a tall but slender plant reaching close to a metre (slightly over three feet) in height. It prefers very wet, even waterlogged sites, growing at the water's edge in sphagnum moss, sometimes with the rhizome under water. The best stands are in western Florida and southern Alabama, and are at their most striking when the new leaves appear among the red flowers.

The pitchers are markedly seasonal in appearance, with relatively few in spring, often some phyllodia formed during summer (especially in drier conditions), and a larger crop of vigorous and particularly colourful pitchers in early autumn. These later pitchers may last in good condition up to early winter in mild climates. The pitcher colours are very variable, usually with a white top veined in green or red, or both. This may partly be due to introgression, as White Pitcher seems prone to hybridisation especially with Pale and Parrot pitchers.

As a result of this variability many cultivars have been named (and lost) in the past, but a comparable diversity can be still be seen in existing stands. In the wild, two distinct pitcher groups are fairly easily recognised, though intermediates between them aren't uncommon. The larger type has a white top veined mainly with green, a large lid and a flared opening. The smaller

∧ S. leucophylla *'Schnell's Ghost'*

∨ S. psittacina *traps from the victim's viewpoint.*

type shows varying degrees of pink to red veining which often spills over into the white areas, and the lid is flexed more upwards. Extreme forms vary from pure white tops with red or pink fringes, to red or pink tubed plants.

The hood has an undulating edge, and the spout is well developed. The inside of the hood is lined with a dense cover of silky hairs; on some plants the entire pitcher may be finely but densely furred. These are often referred to as variety *pubescens*, though this name seems to have no formal botanical status. White Pitcher is very attractive to insects, and the traps may fill up within days of opening, especially in autumn.

The flowers are almost as large as in Yellow Pitcher, and appear from early to middle spring. They are usually a deep, rich red although in the green-and-white mutant 'Schnell's Ghost' (and some other forms) they are a pale greenish-yellow. Another flower mutant with multiple tepals (an undifferentiated mass of sepals and petals) called 'Tarnock' has recently been registered.

Unlike in other *Sarracenia* species, the seed capsule shrivels from the base rather than the tip, apparently an adaptation reducing the likelihood of seed capture by the style umbrella when the mature seeds begin to fall.

PARROT PITCHER *S. PSITTACINA*

SYNONYMS *S.calceolata*, *S. pulchella*.
RANGE From far-eastern Louisiana across southern Alabama and Georgia to the southern tip of South Carolina, also the far northern strip of Florida including all of the panhandle.
DESCRIPTION Parrot Pitcher is perhaps the most aquatic *Sarracenia*, and its various specialisations reflect this. The backward-leaning, parrot-headed traps are immediately recognisable, though the plants are easily overlooked among taller vegetation unless they are in flower. It grows in lower-lying, more flood-prone areas than the other species. If the plant is covered too quickly by accumulating sediments, the rhizome will change to a narrow, fast-growing form which will grow up to the detritus surface before forming new crowns. Because of its small size and low habit this species is particularly vulnerable to fire exclusion, which allows it to be grown over by other plants. It is also unusually shade tolerant, presumably an adaptation for survival under competing plants when fires are infrequent.

The flowers are small at around 5 centimetres (2 inches) across, faintly sweet-smelling, and may appear through much of spring. Flower colour is particularly variable, from the usual red to green and yellow, and with odd plants in some populations having orange, deep pink or even dark red blooms which appear close to black. Parrot Pitcher hybridises readily with other species in their range apart from Yellow Pitcher, producing some interesting results. These hybrids may be slow-growing and not good at capturing prey due to the incompatible form of the very different traps of the parents.

Young pitchers mostly appear in spring, standing upright at first, then drooping backwards as they mature. They are long-lasting, often being in good condition a year or more after opening. The pitchers are fairly variable in colour, shape and size, usually between 10 and 20 centimetres (4 to 8 inches) in length, though much larger pitchers to 30 centimetres (1 foot) are not uncommon in Okefenokee Swamp and southern Mississippi. Florida plants tend to have less-developed hoods than those in the Gulf area. Pitcher colour may vary from all red with white fenestrations, to combinations of red, bronze and pink over green and white; all-green forms have also been recorded recently.

The traps are often compared to those of the Californian Cobra Lily (*Darlingtonia*), and for good reason. However, Cobra Lily has a chromosome count of 30 compared to the 26 of all *Sarracenia*, and produces no digestive enzymes, so this resemblance is more likely the result of convergence than close evolutionary relationships. Also, Cobra Lily pitchers are upright, with the wing twisted 180° as the pitcher rises, an ideal form for guiding terrestrial insects such as ants and beetles up to the deadfall trap. Interestingly, Parrot Pitcher will also trap ants and terrestrial beetles efficiently in drier areas — even though it grows horizontally, not upright.

Parrot Pitcher traps are well adapted to capturing aquatic prey. They have often been described as a lobster pot type trap, but are closer to the more complex and efficient fyke net which is horizontal rather than upright and has a central leading net running up to its funnel mouth, like the very pronounced wing (ala) of Parrot Pitcher. Aquatic animals bumping into the plant's ala tend to turn sideways rather than move up and over. Crustaceans such as cladocerans or copepods are particularly prone to staying at one level, moving up and down only slowly through the day as they follow the light-influenced movements of their minute phytoplanktonic prey.

Many aquatic animals are strongly attracted to light, and those approaching the funnel entrance to the trap are enticed by the bright windows showing within which contrast strongly with the shaded mouth. Once inside, they are unlikely to swim

∧ *Sectioned pitchers: the two above are from* S. psittacina, *below is* Darlingtonia californica.

∨ *Submerged plant of* S. psittacina *surrounded by drifts of water fleas,* Daphnia *and* Moina *species.*

\> S. minor — *an Okefenokee form.*

out again, partly because of the incurved collar

In addition, from inside the hood the entrance is darker than the numerous bright windows. It may be even darker when underwater, as light entering water is already partly polarised into slanting horizontal planes, and the upright ala will mainly transmit vertically polarised light.

Trapped animals are then drawn towards the tube of the pitcher by its particularly large, bright windows. They will be guided down the neck of the pitcher by the numerous thick and long (5-millimetre; one-fifth of an inch) hairs here, all pointed towards the base of the pitcher to prevent an easy return. These gradually come closer together, making return impossible, but not so abruptly that it is difficult for prey animals to start moving in that direction in the first place. In a fyke net, wary animals

such as eels are guided in a similar fashion by a series of funnels, each with a smaller opening than the last.

Prey animals recorded for *S. psittacina* include tadpoles, copepods and cladocerans, and in plants cultivated underwater during warmer months I have also found several types of water bugs, small water beetles, and even water snails. Above water, ants, beetles and sometimes millipedes seem to be the most common prey, the ants being attracted by numerous nectar glands along the ala. Older pitchers may be choked with beetle and ant remains, so an aquatic period in winter does not appear to be important for this species. Flies are rarely found among these remains, although they are common in upright *Sarracenia* species.

Above water, Parrot Pitchers secrete liquid at their bottom end, but it is not known whether this contains digestive fluids. In England, unsubmerged plants are reputedly prone to rot infection by *Botrytis* fungi in winter. This seems strange as they grow well above water throughout the year in other climates, even tolerating freezing to at least −9°C (16°F).

HOODED PITCHER S. MINOR

SYNONYMS *S. adunca*, *S. galeata*, *S. lacunosa* (see comment under White Pitcher) and *S. variolaris*.

RANGE From around the middle of the Florida panhandle to as far south as any pitcher grows, in Okeechobee County in Florida. Also across southern Georgia along the Atlantic coastal plain to southern North Carolina.

DESCRIPTION Across much of its range, Hooded Pitcher is generally found growing in drier places than other *Sarracenia* species, and may even be found in light shade under Longleaf Pines (*Pinus palustris*). It often occurs in small groups that actually may be a single clone which has spread by rhizomes, but in regularly burnt areas it may

S. rubra *subsp.* gulfensis *cultivar 'Velvety Red'.*

form larger and more widely spaced colonies. Most plants reach between 30 and 60 centimetres (1 to 2 feet) under such conditions. However, the largest plants of around 90 centimetres (3 feet) are found in permanently wet places in the Okefenokee Swamp, with their rhizomes floating in sphagnum moss at the edge of streams. Plants transplanted from the wild and cultivated under very wet conditions tend to grow larger than their uncultivated siblings.

Pitchers appear throughout the growing season, and last up to twelve months in mild climates. The back of the pitcher has large, showy white windows like those of Parrot Pitcher, and these probably have the same function. The opening to the pitcher is completely overhung by the wide, domed hood, which makes the back of the pitcher brighter and more attractive to prey. The inside of the mouth is usually a dark red, making the fenestrations look even brighter by comparison. Insects climb up along the ala and lip, which are liberally dotted with nectar glands, in search of nectar. In Florida, over 90 per cent of the recorded prey is ants, as it also is in cultivated plants almost anywhere in the world.

This species is not particularly free-flowering, and seed set is also often poor with only around 100 to 150 seeds per capsule. The fairly small blooms reach around 6.5 centimetres (2.5 inches) across, and are bright yellow and very conspicuous, appearing through much of spring. Unlike in other species, they open at the same time as the new pitchers, or even later. Horticulturists recommend that the rhizomes of this species should be set deeper in the soil than for other species, but I have found this unnecessary if plants are always kept wet.

The only named cultivar to date is 'Dark Ladies', a dwarf clone between 15 and 20 centimetres (6–8 inches) which is unusually red both inside and outside the hood. 'Okefenokee Giant' is not a clone name, but is used loosely to refer to any taller plant specimen from that wetland. Wild hybrids with Parrot Pitcher are not uncommon.

SWEET PITCHER S. RUBRA

OTHER COMMON NAMES Red Pitcher.
SYNONYMS *S. gronovii* var. *rubra*, *S. media*, *S. nigra*, *S. sweetii*. The variety *acuminata* is now regarded as an invalid synonym of subspecies *rubra*.
RANGE This is a complex group of plants, and two 'forms', sometimes separated as species, are described in the next two entries. Plants which are obviously forms of this species are described here. Subspecies *wherryi* is found around the south-eastern tip of Mississippi across southern Alabama and just into western Florida. Florida populations further east (but all in the western panhandle) and those in south-western Georgia are regarded as subspecies *gulfensis*.

However, note that there are some intermediate plants between these subspecies, with populations that are difficult to fit conveniently under any label, and which make it hard to define the subspecies themselves. The typical subspecies *rubra* seems to be more clearly defined geographically, from south-eastern Georgia along the Atlantic coastal plain to southern North Carolina, though plants intermediate between *rubra* and *gulfensis* are known from around central Georgia. Canebreak and Mountain pitchers are treated separately later, to help separate the variants of this complex more clearly.
DESCRIPTION The common name Sweet Pitcher probably derives not only from the floral fragrance, but also from an old scientific synonym *S. sweetii*. It is found in sphagnum bogs growing in moss, as well as on muddy soils and along stream banks, where plants may form dense thickets from the closely packed and very forked rhizomes.

The pitchers are often red, finely veined with a distinctive network unlike that of the other species described earlier, and are often finely pubescent. Spring pitchers of all three subspecies described here are relatively small, and not as upright as those appearing later. By summer and early autumn, larger, more upright and more richly coloured and veined pitchers are formed — these often last through winter in mild areas.

In subspecies *rubra* pitchers reach between 30 and 45 centimetres (12 to 18 inches) high. The spout on the lip is poorly developed, and there is a slight bulge in the upper pitcher below the mouth. The column supporting the hood is short, and the hood itself more or less follows the contour of the mouth when viewed from above. The hood is fairly flat in this subspecies, not wavy-edged, and the flowers are very fragrant. However, there are other variants including a long-lidded form from North Carolina with a lid up to 5 centimetres

S. rubra *subsp.* alabamensis

S. rubra *subsp.* jonesii *These spring pitchers haven't developed their characteristic bulging throat fully.*

(2 inches) long but no wider than the usual forms.

In subspecies *gulfensis* there is a distinct spout, and these plants may reach 50 centimetres (20 inches) high. The lid is relatively large, and wavy-edged. Flowers in this subspecies are not particularly fragrant. These variable plants include stocky variants up to 30 per cent wider than high, and giant variants to as much as 60 centimetres (2 feet) tall at Yellow River in Florida. An all-green form with yellow flowers shows some white marking on its hood, slightly resembling White Pitcher and possibly inheriting this colouration through introgression.

In subspecies *wherryi* the hood is elongate and curved slightly outwards, with a wavy lid which may be tinted red. These plants reach around 30 centimetres (1 foot) generally, except around Chatom, Alabama where they approach twice this height. They are similar to Canebreak Pitcher, but are olive-green rather than yellow-green and more strongly tinted with red on the outside.

Two other Sweet Pitcher subspecies are discussed separately below, partly because a good case can be made for separating them as species in their own right, and also to distinguish them more clearly from the above subspecies.

The flowers of all forms described above are fairly small at around 5 centimetres (2 inches) across, usually red or dark red, and sweetly fragrant, sometimes compared to a rose or fruit. However, even in normally coloured plants flowers may sometimes be yellow, or even orange to pink. They appear around mid to late spring, the densely packed rhizomes and free-flowering plants of mature plants making a spectacular sight in bloom. All of these plants appear to be particularly good at catching wasps, despite their relatively small size.

CANEBREAK PITCHER *S. RUBRA* SUBSP. *ALABAMENSIS*

OTHER COMMON NAMES Alabama Canebreak Pitcher.
SYNONYMS Often treated as a separate species, *S. alabamensis*.
RANGE Central Alabama north of Montgomery, localised in small colonies of which 12 still survive.
DESCRIPTION The pitchers of this variant are usually yellow-green, reaching up to 50 centimetres high (20 inches) with a distinct spout. They are barely marked on the outside, but show prominent red veins inside the throat. However, some plants are markedly red-veined on the outside, and these often turn redder in mid to late summer, with a networked pattern that is similar to more typical *S. rubra*. The pitchers tend to die back in winter, and phyllodia may form in cold climates. The flowers are also similar to those of Sweet Pitcher, usually red, though an orange-flowered clone is known.

Many of the remaining populations of this endangered species are in overgrown and shaded places, where their rhizome growth becomes abnormal with elongated sections appearing above ground. Atlanta Botanical Garden is now managing and restoring some of these sites, using fire after clearing shrubs and other taller plants.

MOUNTAIN PITCHER *S. RUBRA* SUBSP. *JONESII*

OTHER COMMON NAMES Mountain Sweet Pitcher.
SYNONYMS Sometimes treated as a separate species, *S. jonesii*.
RANGE Mainly in a small pocket of North Carolina, near the western boundary of the two Carolinas, but also in one adjacent county of South Carolina.

Mountain Pitcher is even more endangered than the Canebreak Pitcher, remaining in only around nine sites. The main threat to this plant is so-called 'poachers', although I believe this name glamorises profiteering thieves who have stripped entire populations of these protected plants from the wild in recent years, including all wild anthocyanin-free (all-green) forms. Collectors who buy any plants of this, or any, protected species without full CITES documentation are no better than the poachers themselves — they are equally to blame for the destruction of wild populations and are also equally liable to prosecution!

DESCRIPTION It reaches around 60 centimetres (2 feet), sometimes taller, and is the most robust of the *S. rubra* complex. In less than optimal growing conditions the pitchers resemble Sweet Pitcher, but otherwise show a characteristic bulge in their upper part, and the veining is perhaps more purple than red. As would be expected from its high and more northerly range, it is more tolerant of cold than Sweet Pitcher, yet it also dies back in areas with a cold winter like that species.

Mountain Pitcher grows in open grassland, so its habitats were more readily and earlier converted to potato fields, golf courses, or were grazed. It is likely that fire has not been an important factor in its ecology, though it may still be useful as a management tool for some populations which are overgrown with grasses and herbs. These include two populations with significant numbers of all green plants with yellow flowers. The sweet-smelling flowers (some people have compared them to violets when first open) are more commonly red and appear in early summer in the natural range.

S. purpurea: *foreground subsp.* venosa 'All Crimson', *at back subsp.* purpurea *form* heterophylla.

PURPLE PITCHER *S. PURPUREA*

OTHER COMMON NAMES Northern Pitcher Plant, Huntsman's Cup, Sidesaddle Plant, Frog's Britches, Dumbwatches (the last name refers to developing capsules, said to resemble watches without hands).
SYNONYMS *S. gibbosa*, *S. grandiflora*, *S. terra-novae*, *S. viridis*. Subspecies *parviflora* and variety *typica* are synonyms of subspecies *venosa*. *S. aurea* is a synonym of *S. purpurea* subsp. *purpurea* form *heterophylla*, while subsp. *gibbosa* and subsp. *terra-novae* are synonyms of subsp. *purpurea*. Other invalid names under *S. purpurea* ssp. *purpurea* are forms *incisa* and *plena*, and varieties *stolonifera* and *riplicola*.

The recently named *S. rosea* is a synonym of the plant presently known as *S. purpurea* subsp. *venosa* var. *burkii*. It is hard to understand why a new name was published for this plant — it would have been better renamed *S. burkii* if it is to be treated as a separate species. Recent evidence suggests that this plant is sufficiently different genetically from other plants under subspecies *venosa* that it should probably become a subspecies in its own right.

Having spelt out these names in such detail, it is also worth noting a potentially serious nomenclature problem with the naming of subspecies *purpurea* and *venosa* which was resolved just before this book went to press. A close examination of the type of Purple Pitcher has revealed that the northern subspecies should technically be subspecies *gibbosa* (or just possibly even *terra-novae*), and it was the southern subspecies that should correctly be subspecies *purpurea*. As changing these long-used names would have caused immense confusion in the literature for decades to come, a proposal to conserve the presently used and long familiar names (based on a new type specimen) has recently been passed by the appropriate Botanical Congress.

RANGE By far the largest in the genus. The southern subspecies *S. purpurea* subsp. *venosa* (as presently defined) extends from eastern Louisiana (where it is apparently long-extinct) across to north-western Florida, and southern Alabama and Georgia. There is a gap here, then this subspecies (as presently defined) reappears from eastern Georgia along coastal areas to New Jersey, where it overlaps with the northern subspecies, *S. purpurea* subsp. *purpurea*.

The latter subspecies ranges northwards and inland from New Jersey, across to British Columbia in the far west of Canada, and is also naturalised in Scotland, Eire and Sweden. It is the floral emblem of Newfoundland, one of the ten Canadian Provinces.

VARIETIES OF THE SOUTHERN SUBSPECIES *VENOSA*
Variety *venosa* from the Atlantic coastal plain usually has deep red flowers. In the variety *montana* from the southern Appalachians, the hood lobes fold inwards until they are almost touching. Variety *burkii* (perhaps a subspecies in its own right) from the Gulf coastal plain has pale-pink to lavender petals, the centre of the flower is whitish to pale green, and the young pitchers are often very pale. A recently named but rare all-green form of variety *burkii* is called *luteola*.

VARIETIES OF THE NORTHERN SUBSPECIES *PURPUREA*
Form *heterophylla* is a fairly widespread yellow-green variant with no red pigment. It may occur patchily in normal red populations, or even be the dominant form in some places, forming clumps up to 1.5 metres (5 feet) across. Worth mentioning is the form previously described as variety *riplicola*, as this is sometimes used casually to describe brittle plants with short pitchers found in alkaline bogs, a unique tolerance among *Sarracenia*. If transplanted into acid bogs such plants revert to normal subsp. *purpurea* within one to three years, so they are not in any way genetically distinct.

DESCRIPTION Purple Pitcher is an apparent paradox — a *Sarracenia* that doesn't seem very effective as a carnivorous plant, yet the northern subspecies has spread in the wake of melting glaciers after the last ice age, until it ranges over much of Canada and the north-eastern USA. This is also the most studied of all the pitchers, partly because of its wide natural range, and numerous papers on its biology have appeared in recent years throwing new light on its ecology and adaptations.

Southern plants (subsp. *venosa*) are most heat tolerant and can be grown even in the subtropics. These are particularly well adapted to aquatic conditions, and may grow across shallow, slow-moving, acid streams. In such conditions their rhizomes float, becoming long and stringy, with unusually elongated leaves appearing on rhizome sections near the surface. The leaf spacing in such conditions is also unusual, as they are often 5 to 8 centimetres (2 to 3 inches) apart. The same plants growing in sphagnum moss at the side of the stream may be deeply bedded, with only a hole showing where the pitchers open. Not surprisingly, the southern plants are also very shade-tolerant, surviving even among quite dense shrubs in places, and thrive best with a relatively cool root zone and some shading when grown in areas with long, hot summers.

Northern plants (subsp. *purpurea*) are strongly cold-adapted, becoming stunted towards subtropical areas, and are possibly less well adapted to aquatic conditions. Though pitchers buried among sphagnum appear half-submerged, they don't seem to adopt the floating habit of southern plants when growing free in water. Conserving water in their cold, damp, high latitude zones is a lesser problem than in the south, and plants have been recorded as growing even on relatively dry spots on hills. They are also much more tolerant of soil variations, having been recorded on soils from a distinctly acid pH 4 or so to a moderately alkaline pH 8.9.

Sarracenia x 'Tina', possibly an infraspecific hybrid between variants of S. purpurea which do not occur together in the wild, although it may also include some other genes.

EVOLUTION AND ADAPTATION IN THE NORTHERN S. P. SUBSPECIES *PURPUREA* The northern pitcher (subsp. *purpurea*) has long been noted for its inefficiency as a carnivorous plant, but is by far the most successful coloniser among all *Sarracenia* as it has spread across much of Canada and part of the north-eastern USA in perhaps the past fifteen thousand years. Its pitchers are usually full of water, and it has been suggested that this is the only species that drowns prey. However, an accumulating weight of studies on inquiline (living within the pitchers) animal, bacterial and protozoan communities suggests a different role for the pitchers.

Although the 'traps' of the northern pitchers are obviously related to the pitfall-type traps found in most other species, they differ in many significant ways. Their Zone 2 is tiny, a narrow band just above the water level of a full pitcher. Zone 3 (often submerged in this species) was originally described as having glands much like those in the comparable zone of the upright species, but recent high-resolution examination with a scanning electron microscope shows no sign of any such glands.

The pitchers don't produce much in the way of attractants such as nectar, nor are they likely to attract enough prey in these cold regions to justify the energy it would take to create attractants. In some areas more than half the pitchers catch nothing over their two year lifespan, with around 8 per cent of the pitchers catching about 66 per cent of the total prey recorded. That isn't very much in any case — videotapings show that less than 1 per cent of the (uncommon) insect visitors to the pitchers are caught, and spiderwebs reduce this further by closing off as many as 10 per cent of the pitchers.

Yet the plants are obviously vigorous despite these poor capture rates, and apparently conserve most of the energy which would otherwise be wasted on attracting and digesting prey where little is available. Newly opened pitchers produce hydrolytic enzymes for around two weeks after they unfold, but production of enzymes virtually stops after that time if no prey is caught. The plants don't suffer for lack of prey, though: a four-month micronutrient study has shown that captured prey provides only about 10 per cent of the annual require-

ment of nitrogen and phosphorus for northern pitchers. The soils and waters they grow in often contain *more* than the remaining amount needed!

At the same time, the pitchers provide a miniature pond environment which usually hosts a diversity of inquiline life forms and ecologies — these may sometimes be as simple as one or two species of bacteria. The bacterial species vary from one pitcher to the next depending on what predators are also present within the pitcher, but on average are fairly similar within each geographic population.

At least three of these bacteria species are known to fix nitrogen in forms which almost all plants can use directly, and the few prey animals the pitchers manage to catch are broken down by proteolytic and chitinolytic bacteria, which between them can digest almost all insect remains. Still other bacteria are present in many pitchers. These various bacteria are frequently preyed on by more complex life forms including rotifers and protozoans, which in turn are often preyed on by a wide variety of insect larvae, all living together within the pitcher pool.

Some of these larvae make the northern pitcher their specific home, including the mosquito *Wyeomyia smithii* (a related species *W. haynei* is found in the southern subspecies *S. purpurea* subsp. *venosa*). Other predatory or scavenging larvae recorded inside the pitchers include midges, stoneflies, alderflies, caddisflies and sarcophagid flies, the latter being relatives of the prey-robbing species of southern *Sarracenia*. Still other aquatic animals may also be present, particularly minute crustaceans including copepods and cladocerans, as well as rotifers and mites.

Because such communities must be really small to fit, there are usually only a few species at most in any one pitcher. Most of the larger and more predatory species are possibly recent arrivals in evolutionary terms, which have moved into the pitchers for the edible bacteria and other prey already living there. Some of the prey (in any particular pitcher, if not necessarily neighbouring ones) may be driven to extinction by more efficient competition or predation, while others appear in varying proportions depending on what other predators are present. Some of this variable fauna may be absent from pitchers in areas that don't suit them — for example *Wyeomyia* is absent from windy and exposed sites.

Inside the pitcher, the water is oxygen-rich, often more than 77 per cent saturated, apparently mainly diffusing through the walls of the pitcher. At least one of the larvae associated with pitchers is unable to survive at lower oxygen concentrations. There may also be a considerable amount of carbon dioxide present (a waste product of all animals), which combines with water to produce weak carbonic acid. Thus the pH inside the pitcher may vary from an acidic pH 3.1 to around neutral at pH 7.2.

The pitchers themselves produce some oxygen as a result of photosynthesis taking place in the chloroplasts (the organs containing the green, photosynthetic pigment chlorophyll), and like all green plants produce carbon dioxide at night. They even show chloroplast activity in the bottom zone of the pitcher. To be able to do this, the pitchers must direct reasonable amounts of light to their inside, and this is probably another reason they usually hold water to their brim. Water refracts, or 'bends', light downwards into the pitcher, acting as a sort of non-focusing lens. The pitchers are often covered with sphagnum moss so that only their opening is visible, and a water-filled pitcher will collect more light than an empty one under these conditions. The shallower the angle of the incoming light (and this angle will always be relatively shallow in the high latitudes of the northern pitcher), the greater the 'bending' downwards from the water's surface. However, a considerable proportion of this incoming light is also lost by reflection at such shallow angles.

Despite these potentially high light levels, it is interesting to note that no algae have ever been recorded inside any northern pitcher, yet these minute plants can be found in virtually every other aquatic environment worldwide, however small or cold. My own speculation is that the northern pitcher is allelopathic, producing something that discourages algal growth. If confirmed, it could be just what the swimming pool industry has been hunting for decades now!

Continuing studies of these inquiline communities will probably reveal an ever more complex array of species and interactions, probably with many further species as yet unrecorded appearing in so-far unstudied places. What *all* of these species do is produce wastes, often rich in the nutrients all *Sarracenia* require. A recent study has shown that where no predators are present, and the water approaches its preferred acidity of pH 4, the inquiline rotifer *Habrotrocha rosa* may build up to such numbers on its bacterial diet that it *alone* can produce far more surplus nutrient than the plant can use. A related species *H.* cf. *rosa* is common in the southern pitcher subspecies *venosa*.

Why has the northern pitcher evolved so dramatically in this direction, instead of following the predatory pathway of all its relatives? The southern subspecies *venosa* already shows some distinctive adaptations, but I would suggest that the northern forms have evolved so much further because there was virtually no insect prey available at the foot of the glaciers where they evolved and began to spread. The icy bogs formed at the foot of melting glaciers are often shrouded in mist, unlike tundra, which may swarm with a multitude of biting insects for a few short months each summer.

It is this specialisation *away* from the predatory lifestyle and towards a symbiosis with animals that has probably allowed the northern subspecies to spread so rapidly in the wake of the glaciers. There would have been no problem with seed spread, as all *Sarracenia* seed floats, so northern pitchers could easily colonise new bogs as the ice retreated. Retreating glaciers millennia ago may have created exceptionally boggy conditions, as the weight of deep ice sheets may have depressed the Earth's crust by as much as a kilometre (over 3000 feet) in these areas.

Much of Canada and the Great Lakes area is poorly drained, even now — what must it have been like with even less vertical fall for water to drain to the sea? Retreating glaciers in these areas also leave alkaline rock rubble in their wake, and it can take around fifteen years for this to be leached by rain to a level most plants will tolerate. This is probably why the northern Purple Pitcher has become exceptionally tolerant of alkaline soils, an adaptation which would have allowed it to colonise newly formed bogs ahead of most other plants.

The original population of *S. purpurea* subsp. *purpurea* would have originated somewhere in the far south-east of its huge present range (as the rest of this was covered by glaciers eighteen thousand years ago) before spreading north and west. Genetic studies confirm that variation is greater to the south and east, as well as that many northern pitcher populations show relatively little genetic diversity.

To summarise, the Northern Purple Pitcher may rely far more on waste products from the diverse animals which live within its mini-pond environment than on trapping live prey. Coincidentally, it has also developed a tolerance for alkaline soils, which has allowed it to spread in the wake of receding glaciers so that it is now the most widespread *Sarracenia*. Perhaps it should become a role model for our troubled world, a plant-of-prey which has become a home for many other living organisms, and has benefited from them in turn!

Sectioned pitchers of S. purpurea: at left subspecies purpurea, at right subspecies venosa.

part two

SARRACENIA IN CULTIVATION

Flowering plants of S. flava *'Purple Throat'*
and S. leucophylla *in morning sun.*

FROM ICY
GARDEN
TO COOL
GREENHOUSE

Whether grown in pots or in the garden, *Sarracenia* are the easiest of all carnivorous plants to maintain. Apart from special attention to water quality and soil mix, they require no further work than dividing and repotting once they have come close to filling their pots. They will even grow well without division for many years, although their pitchers will diminish in size as they become crowded.

If there is any single rule that the great majority of *Sarracenia* growers follow, it is to buy only cultivated plants. Wild plants (usually poached) are still available occasionally, but carry pests and diseases which often can't be eradicated from a collection without destroying all plants and starting again. By contrast, there is not a single desirable species or hybrid which is not already in cultivation somewhere, though you may need to be patient to obtain plants or seed of some of the newer discoveries.

Sarracenia are usually grown for the beauty of their pitchers, but they also have other uses. Many species (even such small ones as Sweet Pitcher) capture and destroy a wide range of undesirable insects from European Wasps to ants and flies. Mature pitchers may also be used as a cut 'flower'

∧*Purple Pitcher is unaffected by light frosts.*

∨ *European Wasps (and some blowflies) trapped by autumn pitchers of S. rubra.*

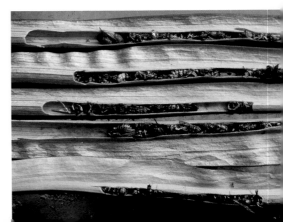

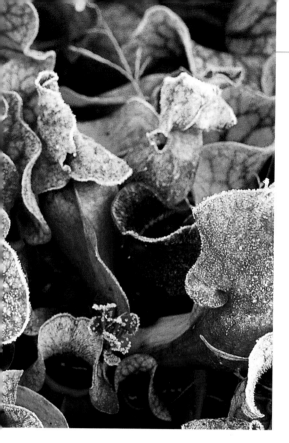

which may stay in good condition for weeks if properly treated — this is discussed in 'Commercial pitcher production'.

The soil, water, temperature, nutrient and light requirements for planting these surprisingly cold-tolerant, temperate zone plants out in the open garden are looked at in this section. Propagation, from basic division to producing your own hybrids, is also covered here, though hybridisation is discussed in more detail in the next section.

CLIMATE AND TEMPERATURE

Many (if not most) *Sarracenia* species and hybrids will survive bitterly cold winters outdoors, particularly if insulated by a thick blanket of snow. In Michigan, an outdoor collection has tolerated blizzards to −27°C (−16°F), while in England a diverse range of species and hybrids was left unaffected by temperatures of −15°C (5°F).

Indeed, *Sarracenia* need a cool to cold rest period, allowing them to go dormant for at least six weeks between 0°C (32°F) and around 10°C (50°F). During this time, dead foliage can be trimmed for best appearance, and also to discourage buildup of pests. Although some growers cut off all foliage, both dead and alive, removing the leaf-like winter phyllodia of Yellow and White Pitchers may reduce the size of pitchers in the following growing season.

In more tropical areas, plants may need to be kept in a refrigerator to allow a dormant period. Three months has been recommended as an adequate period, though this seems excessive, and even if they are slightly frozen at any stage (as sometimes happens to plants just below a freezing compartment) many will recover after a slow thawing period. Drying them out *completely* for two months is also reputed to be an adequate substitute for cold dormancy in tropical areas. In the cooler subtropics (where no special treatment is necessary), plants will come into leaf and flower a little earlier than in more temperate areas. Some will also grow taller than usual, but these look scraggy and unhealthy by the end of their growing season.

Storms during the growing season can be a problem, particularly periods of sleet, hail or rain associated with strong winds. Taller and more upright pitchers may fill with water, but surprisingly few will collapse. There are always some individual pitchers that can't be salvaged after a storm, but most of those which fall will drain themselves, and straighten up within a few hours once the storm passes.

Of the species, both Purple and Parrot Pitchers (and also some of their hybrids) have sometimes been overwintered outdoors under water. However, this is not recommended, and Parrot Pitcher must not be allowed to freeze if kept submerged. At the other extreme, all species will tolerate very high temperatures as well, provided that humidity remains high.

WATER, LIGHT AND FERTILISER

Sarracenia will only grow well with soft water, preferably well below 100 parts per million of dissolved salts. Even at such low levels the salt content will concentrate as the water evaporates, and occasional flushing of potted plants with distilled water, or a period left out in heavy rains, will be necessary to reduce soil salinity.

Deionised or softened waters can't be used as a substitute for distilled water, as these merely swap calcium and sodium ions — both are equally unacceptable for pitcher plants. Chlorinated water also affects growth, but the chlorine can be removed simply by leaving tap water to stand for a day or two before use, or by boiling then cooling if it is needed in a hurry.

All of the species apart from Green Pitcher will grow in wet or waterlogged soils, and even Green Pitcher will thrive in waterlogged conditions through winter and spring. However, if they are grown outdoors in climates where the soil is likely to freeze, dry the soil to barely moist before the first really cold weather sets in. Waterlogged soil has no air spaces in it, and these help to insulate the roots against extremes of temperature.

For best colour, pitcher plants should have at least six hours of sunlight, though they will grow reasonably well with half this amount. In more temperate zones more sunlight is better, but in hot and dry areas 50 per cent shadecloth or the equivalent cover made from slats may be necessary. This is not so much to keep out sunlight, as to maintain higher relative humidity. For the same reason, potted plants in sunny windows should stand in a shallow tray or pot base which is kept full of water at all times.

Fertilisation is easy — don't bother! Outdoor plants will catch all the insects they need for nutrient supply, taking the rest of their needs from sunlight and water as do all other photosynthetic plants. Indoor plants with an adequate supply of insects will also grow well, and you can even feed them additional swatted insects if you like — but not insects which have been sprayed. Overfeeding with fresh insects is impossible.

Indoor plants which have little or no access to insects will need some fertilisation, but very little. There are a few brands of suitably fertilised *Sarracenia* mixes available, and though I have not used any of them, some commercial growers regard them highly. If you prefer to make your own mix but feel some extra fertilisation is necessary, particularly for young plants with pitchers too small to catch much in the way of insects, small amounts of African Violet fertiliser or an equivalent with an NPK ratio of around 10:10:10 will not distort growth visibly.

∧*Potting materials, left to right: river sand, vermiculite, perlite, peat, sphagnum.*

< *The Black Vine Weevil* Otiorhynchus sulcatus *(shown slightly larger than life).*

SOILS

All *Sarracenia* soils are based on peat, and no adequate substitute for this has yet been found. Imitation peats, such as those based on coconut fibre, decay to a slimy mess when kept permanently wet. Peat is a renewable resource, and although peat quarrying has received poor environmental press in recent years this is because much of it is wasted on purposes for which it is not well suited (discussed in 'Commercial pitcher production').

There is no single, ideal mix for *Sarracenia*. Growers use diverse combinations from pure peat to mixes including fine river sand or gravel (marine sands are usually too alkaline), live or dry sphagnum moss (from which much peat is derived), and even vermiculite or perlite. In the interests of economy I prefer to use a mix of 40 per cent river sand and 60 per cent peat, which is heavy when wetted so that potted plants don't topple over in the wind as readily as with lighter mixes.

There are carefully formulated chemical mixes available, which will give good growth rates in ideal conditions. Some growers claim they can produce flowering plants from seedlings in two years using such mixes in a hothouse, but the resulting plants may take years to recover from transplanting outdoors. Some don't survive the move at all.

If using sphagnum, wear rubber gloves and wash your hands after, as it is a potential source of a fungal infection called sporotrichosis. The spores of this disease invade through cuts, and within one to four weeks can cause blisters which inflame and grow. The infection later spreads to the lymph system, often triggering red streaking along the affected arm as an early symptom. If left untreated, the fungus will eventually invade the gut and bones. Peat does *not* harbour this disease.

However, it is essential to never let peat dry out, as it is extremely difficult to wet again afterwards. This is not so hard to avoid in bog gardens, but in warm weather potted plants should be stood in a shallow tray of water which is kept topped up at all times. If you're going away for a week or more during hot weather, stand the pot in a deeper container so it is flooded to the top of the soil. Many species and hybrids will benefit from such treatment throughout the spring and summer, and certainly none will be harmed by it except possibly in frosty weather.

PESTS AND PROBLEMS

If grown as naturally as possible, *Sarracenia* aren't plagued by pests or diseases, and those few problems which appear from time to time will eventually go away of their own accord. Greenfly, tiny winged insects, may appear early in spring on cultivated plants, but usually disappear by late spring. They may persist into summer in a greenhouse (not the perfect environment for *Sarracenia* in any case), in which case they can be lightly dusted with sulphur. Thrips and scale insects may become a serious problem on plants grown indoors or in greenhouses, if not treated at an early stage. These can be controlled with relatively non-toxic treatments such as white oil.

Natural insect pests of *Sarracenia* will inevitably be a problem within the natural range of the species — a good reason to set up commercial plantations outside this range! Collectors should have little trouble removing most insects, as well as spiderwebs blocking off insect supply to some pitchers, by hand. In commercial plantings, spiderweb-clogged pitchers (rarely more than 10 per cent according to the few studies published) will make little difference to overall growth as the other pitchers seem to catch more prey by way of compensation.

The most threatening pest to date is the nocturnal Black Vine Weevil (*Otiorhynchus sulcatus*). The adult weevils are not particularly destructive, but their

CONSTRUCTING A BOG POND

(Top left) Level the edges and line the excavation with wet newspaper or sand.

(Top right) After the liner has been placed, spread a lower water-retaining reservoir of sand, and top with a peat and sand mix.

(Left) The newly-planted pond.

(Below left) Fifteen months later.

(Below right) Two years later.

larvae eat the rhizomes and roots, and later progress to the leaves. The beetle is 2 centimetres (0.8 inches) long with the typical elongated weevil head, and numerous short tufts of yellow bristles over the body.

Infested plants are unlikely to survive once the grubs tunnel into the rhizomes, although it is possible to dig these out if only a few weevils are present. It has attacked *Sarracenia* only in North America, but is a widespread agricultural pest elsewhere. Fortunately the adults cannot fly and must walk from plant to plant, and are therefore controllable through quarantine procedures and careful inspection of new plants.

If you must use an insecticide (for this or any other pest), do so at half strength, though even this may be enough to damage immature pitchers. Insecticides are ineffective on rhizome-eating grubs because they can't easily be applied to the infested site. So-called 'organic' sprays of soapy water, various pyrethrins and even just a very light dusting with wood ash will often do just as good a job on many pests and problems as the more dangerously toxic products. Test these simpler substances on just a few plants at first, hosing them off afterwards with a fine mist of fresh water.

The only other (usually trivial) problem likely to be experienced with *Sarracenia* is bird damage. Some birds will learn to tear out the bottom of insect-filled pitchers and reap the easy harvest within. I know of no cure for this problem, but it is unlikely to develop outside cities and is mostly associated with sparrows, starlings and blackbirds.

CONSTRUCTING A BOG GARDEN

The ideal way to grow the cold-tolerant pitcher plants is in a bog garden, where soil temperatures remain fairly uniform and moisture levels stay constant if the area is watered along with the rest of the garden. These are now usually made from fibreglass or liners varying from the very long-lasting butylene and EPDM membranes, to vari-

ous inexpensive poly and welded sheets. Concrete is more permanent but is harder to work with, and is far from ideal for *Sarracenia* as these plants dislike lime.

With a little care in construction even inexpensive materials such as black plastic sheeting can be used to create a bog garden that will last for decades or even a lifetime. The water-retaining parts of bog garden liners should be *completely* buried, away from the ultraviolet light which rapidly destroys all but the most expensive pond liners, and the exposed edges should be protected and hidden by a rock or tile border.

A soil depth of 15 centimetres (6 inches) is perfectly adequate for vigorous growth, and if you are able to keep up the water supply through most of the warmer months you need not dig deeper than this. However, if you like to get away for a few weeks in summer, 30–40 centimetres would be a better depth. Peat isn't needed in the deeper part which acts mainly as a water reservoir, so sand can be used to fill the liner to around 15 centimetres beneath the surface.

The only difficult part of bog garden construction is making sure that the sides are level to prevent water running out at the lowest edge. Some books recommend puncturing the newly placed liner to prevent waterlogging, but this defeats the purpose of putting it there in the first place and will cost heavily in watering during summer.

Although there are a number of types of inexpensive plastic sheet that can be used underground, some are so flimsy that they would be difficult to lay without damage. Heavier black plastic sheets are available in a wide range of widths and lengths and are more than adequate for most bog gardens. These can be doubled up for additional strength, and their colour doesn't matter because they will be hidden from view.

Liner size should fit the length and width of the excavation, *plus* twice the depth of the hole in each direction, *plus* a bit more to allow for errors especially if the bog garden is an irregular shape. It must be laid carefully (unrolled rather than dragged into position) over a blanket of fine, wet sand 5 centimetres (2 inches) deep, or over wads of wet newspaper which are easier to keep in place on the sloping sides. Even this protective layer may not be enough unless you have first removed all sharp or lumpy objects from the soil below.

Avoid walking on the liner while placing it. If you must do so, wear smooth-soled shoes or go barefooted, as treads often pick up hard or sharp things. If the sides will be steep or the soil is soft and crumbly, work one part cement powder per ten parts soil into the first 5–7 centimetres (2–3 inches) of soil around the sides before putting in a liner. Although this reinforced earth is not as strong as cement, it will be more than firm enough to prevent slippage.

A *Sarracenia* bog doesn't need to be specially screened or placed to be included as part of a more conventional garden. As long as the pond itself is designed in keeping with the overall design of the garden, and multiple plantings of a limited range of favourite pitcher plants are used, it can be fitted harmoniously into most formal or semi-formal gardens.

These striking plants have rarely been used in more formal settings, despite their potential as bold sculptural elements. This neglect is because it is only in recent years that designers have begun to realise how extremely cold-tolerant most *Sarracenia* species and hybrids are.

OTHER PLANTS FOR SARRACENIA PONDS

There is a diverse range of other water- and peat-loving plants that make ideal companions for *Sarracenia*, far too many to list here. The best sources for these are alpine garden specialists, but there are also a few other hardy or semi-hardy carnivores which will thrive outside. Of these, the Venus Flytrap (*Dionaea muscipula*) is most widely available, and is reasonably cold tolerant. In areas with marked frosts it is probably best kept in a pot buried in the soil mix and brought inside before the first freeze.

This method can also be used for carnivorous plants with even greater cold sensitivity such as the various Forked Sundews (all variants of *Drosera binata*) and Cape Sundew (*D. capensis*). In places where frosts are intermittent and light, both of these will be happy outside all year.

PROPAGATION BY DIVISION

Producing new plants by division is easy — any rhizome section with a growing tip and healthy roots can be cut off and replanted. This is usually done from around late winter through spring, though at my nursery in southern Australia I have taken divisions at most times of year with only occasional casualties.

A large clump split into small pieces in this way will usually produce far too many pieces to repot or even give away. As it will

< Dionaea muscipula

> *The pitcher plants are spectacular to look at, but their pond doesn't seem out of place seen in the context of the rest of the garden.*

also take years for any single piece to grow into a specimen plant again, collectors often prefer to thin out surplus rhizome sections rather than splitting up a large plant completely. Eventually, an overgrown pot full of pitchers will end up too choked to grow attractively no matter how much trimming is done, but if smaller pieces have been established years before, these will have formed specimens in the meanwhile.

If numerous divisions are wanted, cutting at about 4–6 centimetres (1.5–2.5 inches) intervals along the rhizomes of larger species will often trigger dormant buds into growth. The cuts should be from the top downwards to around one-third to one-half the thickness of the rhizome. New plants may take up to a year to appear after cutting, and should not be separated until each establishes its own root system.

> Sarracenia seed cold-treated outdoors in a floating tray which keeps the pots partly submerged. The raised glass top stops the seed from being splashed around by rain, and also allows ample air circulation so the seed tray does not turn into a hot-house on sunny days.

v Drosera binata variety extrema

PROPAGATION FROM SEED

Fresh *Sarracenia* seed is easy to germinate, as long as it has been wetted and kept below 5°C (41°F) for 6 to 8 weeks. It is the wetting which is the greatest problem for any method of seed germination for this genus. *Sarracenia* seeds have a rough surface, and are very water-repellent, so it takes time for them to absorb enough water to allow growth to begin.

Usually, seed can be wetted by planting on a saturated, peat-based mix which is sealed in plastic to keep humidity up, and then refrigerated for up to two months. The seed should be sprinkled over the surface rather than buried, as it needs light to trigger germination. It is often suggested that even five-year-old seed can be readily germinated in this way, but the older the seed is, the harder it is to get moisture back into it.

I have rarely had problems with seed less than a few months old, but bought seed treated in the same way often fails to germinate. Wetting agents such as a few drops of detergent can be used to increase absorption, but even this will not reliably improve germination. A further problem is that most seed suppliers don't specify or even necessarily know when the seed was collected, or how it was stored, so it may be dead before the purchaser tries to grow it.

Other suggested methods of encouraging germination in older seed include soaking it for up to a week in a very dilute gibberellic acid solution, a growth stimulant used at the rate of 1 gram of powder per litre (one part per thousand) of water. This is expensive so few small scale growers would want to try it, but 10 millilitres (2 teaspoons) of this solution should be enough to treat around a hundred seeds.

Freezing seeds in water for 48 hours is also reported to trigger germination, though the hygrophobic seeds don't seem to absorb water any better through this treatment. I have found neither this method nor gibberellic acid treatment markedly better than the two-month cold storage technique. It is likely that old or poorly stored seed is the most frequent germination problem, as 70–90 per cent germination is fairly normal when sowing fresh seed.

Timing for seed raising is important. Natural germination is generally in early to mid spring, so the cold treatment should finish around that time. If you live in a cold temperate area, a fridge isn't necessary — sow seed in autumn and leave it to germinate naturally.

The first tiny plants should start to appear after around two to four weeks of warm weather, though this will be slower if temperatures are often low in that time, and some seeds take even longer to sprout. These plantlets should be left to grow for as long as two years before separating and repotting them. Remove any mosses that may grow so they don't smother the seedlings.

Most seedlings will take five to eight years to reach maturity from germination, depending on the species or the ancestry of the hybrid. Some can be forced to grow faster than this, although they will take longer to adapt to outdoor conditions later. But is it worth raising seedlings in the first place? There are probably tens of thousands of different species and hybrid clones already in cultivation.

Certainly, a species collector must learn to raise hand-pollinated seedlings — tearing up wild plants is not acceptable, and the tiny amount of seed needed to bring new populations into cultivation should have little impact on the surviving natural populations of most species and forms. However Green Pitcher, Mountain Pitcher, Canebreak Pitcher

and the montane variety of Purple Pitcher are seriously depleted or limited in range, and are completely protected by law. For these, collectors should be concentrating on preserving genetic variability already in cultivation, both by vegetative propagation and by hand pollinating to produce new generations before older clones die out.

Even casual collectors should try raising some seedlings of their own if only to see how easily it can be done, and to learn how satisfying it is to watch them grow. And of course, hybridisers have no choice but to learn hand pollination techniques.

HAND POLLINATION

Whether you hope to build up genetically pure stocks from populations lost from the wild for reintroduction, or for state-of-the-art hybridisation, the basic hand-pollinating techniques are exactly the same. From both perspectives, raising randomly pollinated seedlings produces the same result — mainly rubbish plants which take up years of your time, effort and space to grow.

The purpose of hand pollination is simple: to produce genetically pure seeds from two particular parents, whether these are closely related clones from

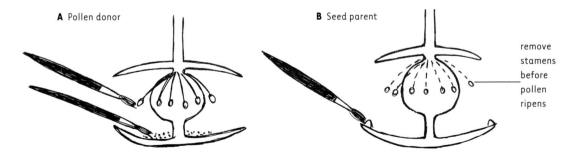

Hand pollination. Pollen can be collected directly from the stamens or the floor of the style umbrella where it falls (A), and is applied to the stigmata (B). Both donor and parent plants must be isolated from other pollen sources at all times.

within the same wild population, or two outrageously different-looking hybrids. In either case, it is mainly the combination of the parent plants which is important.

Floral parts and pollination of *Sarracenia* have already been described in 'History, habitat and function'. Hand pollination is just a way of making sure that only pollen from selected plants makes its way to the equally selected female plants. To avoid fertilisation from any other source, the flowers of both the pollen donor and the seed parent must be screened from pollen-carrying insects. A loose bag of fine cheesecloth or other finely woven cloth tied around both of them just before they open will do this.

If both donor and seed flowers open at the same time there is no problem transferring pollen to the seed parent using a fine brush (which must be sterilised for further cross-pollinations), or a disposable cotton bud, or even a fingertip. This isn't always so straightforward because different species and hybrids may flower months apart. However, pollen can be refrigerated for up to six weeks, or frozen for up to eight weeks if two clones to be crossed have very different flowering times.

To make pollen collection and transfer easier, remove all five of the petals to expose the internal structure of the flower. The seed-producing flower should be rewrapped with the same fine-mesh cloth after hand pollination, so that it can't be re-fertilised by insects bringing in random pollen. Each hand-pollinated, seed-bearing pod should have a tag attached to its stem immediately, including all relevant details on the pollen donor used.

Every flower on the seed-bearing parent can be hand pollinated separately, so a large clump with thirty or more flowers could be hand pollinated by thirty or more other clones, whether these are closely related individuals or selected hybrids. If both parents are from the same wild population, the 30 000 or more seeds which could be produced by carefully managed hand pollination could potentially retrieve nearly all the genes of that population for restoration projects.

The hybridiser's aims are vastly different from the conservationist's, yet all record keeping and overall planning must be carried out just as carefully as for the most localised species-recovery programs. Generally, some excellent hybrid plants will appear in every random bunch of hybrid seedlings, but the best results in the future will increasingly be the result of carefully planned hand pollination.

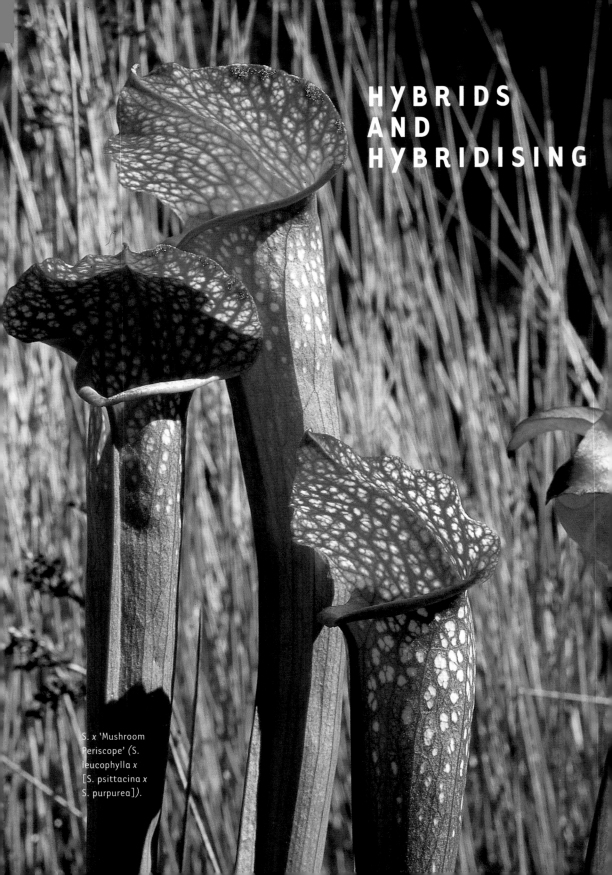

S. x 'Mushroom
Periscope' (S.
leucophylla x
[S. psittacina x
S. purpurea]).

All *Sarracenia* species and their diverse forms hybridise readily, giving fertile offspring that will cross just as readily with any other species or hybrids. This means that there is potentially no end to the possible hybrids that can be created over time, although many are intriguing rather than beautiful — hence Peter D'Amato's elegant expression 'vegetable gargoyles'.

Others can be crossed repeatedly to incorporate upright habit, large size, intense colouration, cold tolerance, unusual vigour, or a long growing season — ideal qualities for the cut pitcher market as discussed in the next section. Collectors and gardeners often want to go in the other direction, breeding smaller plants with each generation from the array of diminutive plants already available.

Whichever direction any hybridiser wants to go, there can be no doubt that we have only begun to skim the surface even just for direct crosses between two species. New colour, size and growth variants of many species are still being introduced into cultivation, giving us the chance to remake early hybrids with better matched parents than were available in the past. Striking hybrid plants can also still be found in the wild, for example the recently named 'Adrian Slack' (probably a variant of *S. x moorei*) with substantial white-capped and rich-red patterned pitchers.

More importantly, complex hybrids potentially offer more and more combinations of specially desirable features, though we will have to raise great numbers of seedlings to find the best combinations of good looks, cold or heat tolerance, long life as cut pitchers, colour, etc. Even a single group of seedlings raised from the same batch of complex hybrid seed produces potentially hundreds of reasonably similar looking but differently behaving seedlings.

Pollination and seed raising were discussed in the previous section, the main difference between raising pure seed and hybrid seed being the choice of parent plants. A more subtle difference is also important — understanding what we hope to achieve through hybridisation and how it can be done, before putting decades of work into collecting, cross-pollinating and creating even more spectacular plants than this already striking genus has to offer.

S. alata 'Red Throat' has been used widely in hybridisation because of its rich throat colouration.

NATURAL HYBRIDS

Wherever two or more wild *Sarracenia* species grow together, and their flowering times overlap at all, there will likely be some natural hybrids. Many of these primary hybrids (that is, direct crosses between two species) have long been known from such natural crosses and because of their distinctive appearance were often thought to be separate species in their own right. Around twenty natural crosses are known, and many of their old binomial names are still widely used, but their hybrid status is now made clear by using an 'x' before the second name.

The most widespread hybrid is the cross of Yellow (*S. flava*) and Purple Pitcher (*S. purpurea*), known as

PRIMARY HYBRIDS OF WILD *SARRACENIA* SPP. WITH PARENT NAMES AND SYNONYMS

Primary hybrid	Parent cross	Synonyms
S. x ahlesii	*S. rubra* x *S. alata*	
S. x alava	*S. flava* x *S. alata*	
S. x areolata	*S. leucophylla* x *S. alata*	
S. x catesbaei	*S. flava* x *S. purpurea*	*S. catesbyi, S. patersonii, S. stevensii, S. atkinsoniana, S. wilsonii, S. porphyroneura, S. elbiana, S. williamsii*
S. x chelsonii	*S. purpurea* x *S. rubra*	
S. x courtii	*S. purpurea* x *S. psittacina*	
S. x crispata	*S. flava* x *S. psittacina*	
S. x excellens	*S. leucophylla* x *S. minor*	*S. x cantabridgiensis*
S. x exornata	*S. purpurea* x *S. alata*	*S. x exoniensis*
S. x formosa	*S. minor* x *S. psittacina*	*S. x decora, S. x maddisoniana*
S. x gilpini	*S. rubra* x *S. psittacina.*	
S. x harperi	*S. flava* x *S. minor*	*S. x crispata* (not to be confused with *S. crispata* which is a synonym of *S. alata*)
S. x mitchelliana	*S. leucophylla* x *S. purpurea*	*S. x patersoniana, S. x tolliana, S. x wilsoniana*
S. x moorei	*S. leucophylla* x *S. flava*	*S. x brucei, S. x mandana, S. x mooreana*
S. x popei	*S. flava* x *S. rubra*	
S. x psittiata	*S. psittacina* x *S. alata*	
S. x readii	*S. leucophylla* x *S. rubra*	*S. x farnhamii*
S. x rehderi	*S. rubra* x *S. minor*	
S. x swaniana	*S. purpurea* x *S. minor*	*S. x flambeau*
S. x wrigleyana	*S. leucophylla* x *S. psittacina*	

S. x catesbaei, which can form large and vigorous clumps. These vary considerably depending on the colouration and size of the two parents, but are usually distinctly red or heavily red-veined. Many other names have also been applied to this hybrid (see above) because it is found almost everywhere that the two parent species grow together, and these are the two most wide ranging plants in the genus.

Primary hybrids and their currently accepted names are listed in the table above with synonyms. It is not usually regarded as important in which order the parents of primary *Sarracenia* hybrids are placed, as the offspring are more or less halfway between their parents in shape, colour, size and other special characters. Technically, the first name listed should be the seed producer, and the second the pollen source, but this is only significant in plant groups where the resulting hybrids may have very different qualities depending on which plant is seed parent, and which is pollen donor.

Primary hybrids were also made in cultivation from an early stage, starting with *S. x moorei* (*S. flava* x *S. leucophylla*) at Glasnevin Botanical Gardens in Ireland,

S. x moorei in the wild. Note how sparsely these pitchers grow compared to cultivated plants.

SOME PRIMARY HYBRIDS ALSO FOUND IN THE WILD

(Top left) S. x mitchelliana

(Top right) S. x wrigleyana

(Left) S. x popei *'Heavily Veined'*

(Below) S. x courtii

PRIMARY HYBRIDS OF *SARRACENIA* SPP. PRODUCED IN HORTICULTURE, WITH PARENT NAMES AND SYNONYMS

Primary hybrid	Parent cross	Synonyms
S. x milata	S. alata x S. minor	S. x miniata
S. x mineophila	S. alata x S. oreophila	
S. x mixta	S. oreophila x S. leucophylla	
S. x pureophila	S. oreophila x S. purpurea	

around the early 1870s. This first cultivated hybrid was named after Dr David Moore, Director of the gardens for over forty years up to 1879, who began the garden's collection of *Sarracenia* (which also led to their introduction into the wild in Ireland — to the regret of some, and pleasure of others). However, the person who actually carried out the cross-pollinations was probably gardener William Keit (Julius Wilhelm Keit) — an early example of how chief executives wave wands and claim the rewards for doing so, while their underlings do the work that actually matters.

OTHER PRIMARY HYBRIDS

Not all primary hybrids can be found in the wild — Canebreak and Mountain pitchers are isolated from all other *Sarracenia* so they can't hybridise naturally, and while Green Pitcher does occur with Sweet Pitcher at one site, they don't seem to flower there at the same time so natural hybrids aren't known. However, various primary hybrids which can't happen naturally *have* been bred by collectors — not all of these have been named, but the named ones are listed in the table above.

S. oreophila x S. psittacina, an unnamed primary hybrid which does not occur in the wild

BREEDING COMPLEX HYBRIDS

All *Sarracenia* are completely cross-fertile, and their hybrid offspring can be bred against each other or against other species for generation after generation. The characteristics of more complex hybrids aren't inherited as predictably as in the primary crosses. On average, they will fall more or less between the appearance of both parents.

However, as genes are mixed in unpredictable ways during fertilisation, some seedlings (in *every* batch raised from the same cross) may look or act more like one or another of their four grandparents, or an unexpected mix of a couple of grandparents. This mixing and matching doesn't just apply to appearance, but to other qualities as well, including when pitchers grow, how long they last, and to some degree how well they catch prey.

They don't necessarily interact together in simple ways, either. It is obvious that all *Sarracenia* species are closely related, or they wouldn't interbreed so freely — and in all later hybrid combinations too. And they are far more closely related than humans and chimpanzees, where roughly 1 per cent genetic difference starting from perhaps five to seven million years ago has caused such massive divergence that there is not the slightest chance of interbreeding, unless a batch of mad scientists decides it would be a wonderful idea to do it artificially.

What this suggests is that the visible differences between what we call *Sarracenia* species may be relatively minor, perhaps programmed by just a very few genes here and there which change the overall shape of a plant by making a whole *range* of other genes work in a new but mutually consistent way. This concept is already fairly well understood if not proven (particularly in mammals), but does not seem to have been applied to plants much even though plant genes, hybridisation, and other interactions are usually much more fluid than in the supposedly 'higher' organisms!

Such pronounced yet basically simple interactions would explain why complex *Sarracenia* hybrids often grow in unexpected ways that don't reflect the exact genetic proportions of their ancestors. Instead, some genes may cancel each other out, interfere with each other, or simply not do anything if blended together.

There is more than a little evidence that such unpredictable genetic interactions happen within *Sarracenia;* for example, the complex hybrids called *S. x willisii* which don't grow as you might expect if the parental genes really did obey the law of averages (this hybrid is discussed later in this section). Yet the *S. x willisii* hybrid has been made repeatedly from different stocks, and the resulting plants are consistently different from what theory would predict.

To simplify the genetic puzzle, think of the genes of each of the four grandparents of a second-generation cross as a jigsaw puzzle of a hundred pieces — though in reality there are many thousands. Some decide the pitcher growing season, others particular colours or patterns, still others shape and posture. Some control a whole range of things, and may not work well together.

In the first cross (between each pair of grandparents), half the pieces available are donated to each seedling, and half are lost — but for that seedling only, because many of its siblings from the same cross will carry a different combination of genetic pieces from the two plants being bred together. Even so, the first generation of crossed seedlings will usually be fairly uniform in appearance and many other qualities.

By the next cross, assuming this is between two completely unrelated first generation hybrids, the situation becomes much more complex, because so many more combinations of pieces can be created or lost. Each second-generation seedling potentially carries a quarter of the pieces

S. x 'Copper Vase', a
hybrid of unknown
ancestry.

from each of the four grandparents, though many will carry more from some grandparents, and fewer from others.

This isn't necessarily obvious though, as all *Sarracenia* are probably closely enough related that the majority of their genes are either the same, or very similar. Some will carry the short pitcher season of one grandparent, some a late growing habit from another, some the strong colour or distinctive pattern of another. A very few may result in novel colour and pattern combinations unlike any of their ancestors.

The more seedlings are raised to a reasonable size from such a cross, the more combinations (both desirable and less so) will be raised. There are two practical consequences. Firstly, most will not be as good as others no matter what your breeding goal may be — these should be mercilessly disposed of as soon as you are sure they aren't among the best.

The second consequence is that some very few second-generation hybrids will inherit a complete range of particularly good or attractive qualities all in the one genetic package, including fast growth as well as a long growing season. The few that do are the supermodels of the *Sarracenia* world, but unlike human supermodels, their attractiveness and vigour may last a century or more. Somewhere in between the poor and the excellent plants lie many other worthwhile varieties.

In the long term, breeding from select supermodel versions would be a mistake. Even the best of these are likely to carry some hidden undesirable, weak or even outright defective qualities, and centuries of misplaced effort in everything from poultry to peas, or maize to merinos have shown that inbreeding destroys long-term vigour in almost every case. Backcrossing to a wide range of vigorous parents, not far removed from wild generations, preserves genetic variability even among hybrids.

It would also be a serious mistake to start from scratch for many of the hybrids that have already been created. For all the present availability of fine new clones of wild plants, some excellent hybrid clones were created a long time ago, many of these from now-extinct wild populations. The preservation of existing hybrids should be a priority for any plants with desirable features, and the best of these are likely to contribute significantly to the hybrids of the future.

The ultimate source of genetic variability is wild plants, of which there are few enough left already. Maintaining healthy wild populations is therefore desirable even for the most one-eyed hybridiser, because this maintains the potential to introduce new 'blood' occasionally from a diverse range of healthy populations with known qualities, seasonality and growth habits.

SPECIES PROPERTIES FOR CROSS-BREEDING

Species and wild populations are the source and the keystone of *any* long-term hybridisation programs in *Sarracenia*, and this is discussed more fully in the next section. It is impossible to guess what uses future generations will have for *Sarracenia* — perhaps a hybrid to target particular pests such as wasps? — though we can be sure they will draw minimally on wild plants.

Whatever properties may be needed, it is the qualities of the species that are central to further hybridisation, and these are considered briefly below.

YELLOW PITCHER The largest (and often tallest) of the species, lending its size and often a fair degree of vigour to its hybrid offspring. Many of the earlier hybrids of this species started from the widespread yellow or green forms, and it is only in recent decades that the rich-red and very heavily veined variants have become widely available, as well as a few of their hybrids.

These give the potential for breeding really large cut pitchers, either heavily veined and patterned or deep red depending on the other parent chosen.

PALE PITCHER Despite its common name this variable species includes forms with intensely coloured mouths and hoods, with others approaching black over much of their tube. Crossed with some of the near-black hybrids such as 'Night Sky', these should give vigorous, upright, often tall plants strikingly patterned over velvety-black. Pale Pitcher has many other unusual, possibly introgressed variants (see 'History, habitat and function') in the wild, and many of these potentially complement other upright species and hybrids. In effect, nature has probably taken a hand here and created diverse and subtle hybrids which would take a breeder a lifetime to repeat.

∧ S. leucophylla x S. oreophila

∨ S. psittacina, *one of various crimson forms which could be used to introduce richer colour into hybrids.*

GREEN PITCHER Although this plant is like a smaller, not very bright Yellow Pitcher in many of its forms, most of its hybrids are exceptionally fast growing, a quality often carried over to the next hybrid generation. New cultivated variants, particularly the highly coloured Sand Mountain forms and some other strongly veined types, are ideal for breeding with other richly veined species. Their offspring will combine vigour and intense patterning, often over a pale background.

WHITE PITCHER These striking, white-topped and upright pitchers with many vein variations from fine and pure-green, to thick and red have long been a favourite for hybridisation. Pitchers of the wild plants tend to be sparsely produced in two short growth spurts, but this problem disappears in many of the hybrids. Backcrossing any White Pitcher hybrid to its parent (or better still, a similar but not closely related clone) will often preserve hybrid vigour as well as the intense white of the upper pitcher. If the other plant used to create the primary hybrid is also strongly veined, the contrast is often very striking.

PARROT PITCHER Although usually small and lying almost on the soil, the distinctive shape of this species creates some very attractive hybrid pitcher shapes. The primary hybrids tend to be too backward leaning to be useful as cut pitchers, but when these hybrids are crossed again with larger, more upright species the distinctive head and rich colouration are often retained on reasonably upright pitchers. Many of the widely available hybrids from this species were bred from small clones of this species, but giant variants in both green and red are becoming available, and should speed up blending this species into commercial-sized hybrids. Parrot Pitcher produces relatively few seeds, and is best used as a pollen donor.

HOODED PITCHER The distinctive hood shape and often prominent windows make this a striking plant for hybridisation, particularly if giant, bronze Okefenokee strains are crossed with other upright and strikingly coloured or patterned species. For cutting purposes, many such crosses are sufficiently close-mouthed that their fine internal colour can't be seen, but this is rarely a problem by the next hybrid generation. This species is usually a poor seed producer, and will produce many more hybrid plants if used to pollinate other species instead.

SWEET PITCHER For hybridisation purposes, this species and Mountain and Canebreak Pitchers can be considered as very diverse colour and pattern variations on a single theme, most of them lending their hybrid offspring a rich and lacy fishnet pattern of red veins. Where this is undesirable (for example, in breeding for green or relatively unpatterned pitchers) the Canebreak Pitcher can be used to produce more golden and less patterned pitchers. Sweet Pitcher itself varies considerably in size

S. x 'Skywatcher', possibly a variant of S. x umlauftiana with pitchers which last well as cut flowers.

parents, and many are relatively upright with wide open, flaring hoods. A second hybrid generation produced against more upright species will often retain the flaring mouth to some degree, plus some hybrid vigour. The northern subspecies *purpurea* gives tighter and less flaring pitchers, also lending its offspring greater cold tolerance. By contrast, the southern subspecies *venosa* gives a more dramatic and flaring hood and the potential to produce hybrids that will thrive in the subtropics without special treatment.

NAMING COMPLEX HYBRIDS

The use of scientific names for natural hybrids seems to have created a fashion for latinised names for complex hybrids, and the best known of these are summarised in the table below. None have much botanical use, and they are probably best ignored as a nomenclatural hiccup from the past. Japanese names have not been included here, as it has never been clear whether these were intended as formal names for all related species crosses, or were intended as cultivar names only.

Other names along these lines can't easily be separated: the so-called *S.* x *caroli-schmidtii* is a cross between *S.* x *chelsonii* and *S. purpurea*, while *S.* x *vittata* is the same cross in the opposite order. Similarly,

from tiny, all-red plants to Chatom giants well suited to cut pitcher breeding. Growers from more temperate areas may want to use Mountain Pitcher to introduce its relative cold hardiness along with the veining pattern of this group. Despite their small size, subspecies *rubra* and *gulfensis* are excellent traps for European Wasps.

PURPLE PITCHER The recumbent habit makes this plant hard to use for cut pitcher production, but its hybrids can reach a large size. They also often carry the deep reds and conspicuous, marbled veins of their

SOME WELL-KNOWN NAMES OF COMPLEX HYBRIDS BETWEEN A SPECIES AND A HYBRID

Primary hybrid	Parent cross	Synonyms
S. x *comptoniensis*	S. *alata* x S. x *willisii*	
S. x *diesneriana*	S. *flava* x S. x *courtii*	
S. x *illustrata*	S. *flava* x S. x *catesbaei*	
S. x *kauffmanniana*	S. *purpurea* x S. x *chelsonii*	
S. x *melanorhoda*	S. *purpurea* x S. x *catesbaei*	S. x *wilmottae*
S. x *sanderiana*	S. *leucophylla* x S. x *readii*	
S. x *superba*	S. *leucophylla* x S. x *excellens*	

SOME NAMES OF HYBRIDS BETWEEN COMPLEX HYBRIDS

Primary hybrid	Parent cross	Synonyms
S. x *laschkei* (or *luschkei*?)	S. x *courtii* x S. x *moorei*	
S. x *schoenbrunnensis*	S. x *courtii* x S. x *exulta*	S. x ?*exculpa*
S. x *umlauftiana*	S. x *courtii* x S. x *wrigleyana*	
S. x *vetteriana*	(S. *alata* x S. x *catesbaei*) x S. x *catesbaei*	
S. x *vogeliana*	S. x *courtii* x S. x *catesbaei*	
S. x *westphalii*	(S. x *mitchelliana* x S. x *moorei*) x S. *leucophylla*	

it is hard to decide whether S. x *exulta* or S. x *exsculpta* is the 'correct' name for S. *purpurea* x S. x *harperi*. None of these crosses appears to be dated — an essential part of formal botanical naming — though it is not clear whether any would have formal status even if they *were* to be properly described and dated.

Some names for still more complex hybrids are shown in table above.

Somewhere along the way, these contrived names have lost any meaning they had in the first place. The more complex the mix of ancestors in a hybrid, the less predictable the appearance of the offspring will be. For example, the complex hybrid S. x *willisii* has been said to be bred from S. x *courtii* against S. x *melanorhoda*. Breaking this down to make sense of what we have here, this is equivalent to (S. *purpurea* x S. *psittacina*) crossed with ([S. *flava* x S. *purpurea*] x S. *purpurea*). In fractions, any plant called S. x *willisii* should be one quarter S. *psittacina*, one eighth S. *flava*, and five eighths S. *purpurea*.

Several writers have pointed out that with this mix of genes, plants called S. x *willisii* shouldn't look as upright and slender as they do. However, there are a number of independently bred clones of this hybrid which are markedly similar. As any complex hybrid may throw back to any of its parents or grandparents in unexpected ways, S. x *willisii* may just be a particularly good example of how unpredictable the appearance of complex hybrids can be.

Whatever future generations may decide to think of the names for complex hybrids, there is certainly no reason to add to them. In future, *Sarracenia* hybrids should be registered by cultivar names, just as for most other groups of cultivated hybrid plants. There is no reason why the ancestry of such cultivars can't be included in their original description as well, but otherwise this sort of information should be shared only between consenting collectors.

NAMING & REGISTERING CULTIVARS

The formal process of naming *Sarracenia* cultivars is really only just beginning. Basically, all new cultivar names must now be described and published in a modern language, with a high quality colour photo of the plant described, or they will have no official status.

There are two main groups of cultivars for *Sarracenia*: those that are variants of a species, and hybrids. If the new plant is a distinctive form of a species, whether grown from wild seed or from a cross made between different clones of the species in cultivation, the cultivar

name must include the species name. For example *S. leucophylla* 'Schnell's Ghost' has long been known in cultivation, while *S. leucophylla* 'Crimson Snow' is a recently named seedling which first appeared in an earlier book of mine.

Variants of S. x willisii 'Pink Windows', (above left) with no white showing and (below) the white-marbled 'Broad Lid'. S. x 'Turtle Mouth' (above right), ([S. purpurea x S. psittacina] x S. rubra).

The same naming procedure can also apply to primary hybrid crosses with Latinised names which have long been in use, for example the many forms of *S. x excellens* or *S. x catesbaei* (though few of these have been given individual cultivar names to date). However, cultivar names for hybrid crosses could also be published more simply — for example *S. x* 'Night Sky'. These more compact names are particularly appropriate for complex hybrids, although the ancestry of such plants should be included with the description if it is known.

Cultivar names can only be applied to the specific plant first described under a name, or to divisions or tissue-cultured plants taken from that plant. They cannot be applied to *any* other plant, no matter how similar it may look.

Descriptions of new cultivars may be published in any appropriate journal or book, although the International Carnivorous Plant Society encourages publication in the *Carnivorous Plant Newsletter*. Whether this will continue to be feasible in this relatively small, quarterly journal (also publishing scientific papers, grower's accounts and descriptions for all other carnivorous plant groups, not just *Sarracenia*) remains to be seen, although at present only commercial growers seem eager to register their better new varieties.

part three

SARRACENIA AS CUT 'FLOWERS'

A vase of mixed Sarracenia pitchers used as cut flowers.

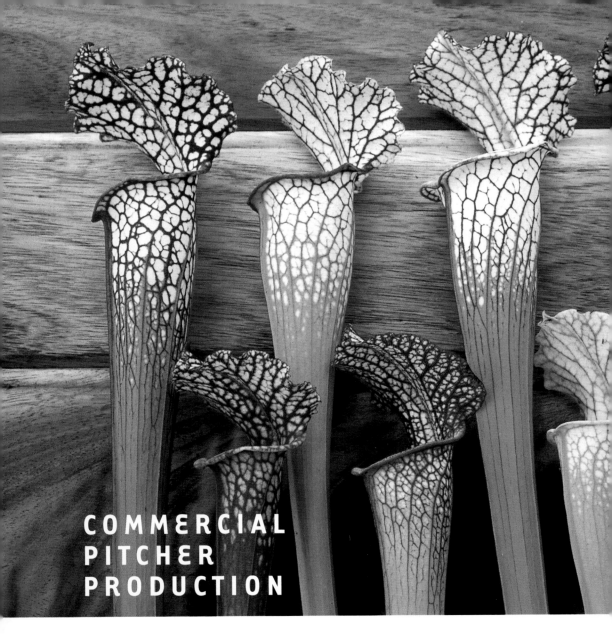

COMMERCIAL PITCHER PRODUCTION

Many types of *Sarracenia* pitchers can be used as long-lasting cut 'flowers' if kept in a cool place — a vase in front of me as I write includes some cut five weeks ago, though this longevity is exceptional. In the USA several million wild-harvested White Pitchers are sold every year, and growers in Honduras are setting up to produce cultivated pitchers for the same markets.

The production potential for cut pitchers is much greater than this, particularly using a diversity of faster-growing and particularly colourful hybrids. Commercial plantings could succeed in most of the warmer temperate zones of the world, and many hybrids will thrive even in cold temperate areas if protected by a thick blanket of snow in winter.

The most suitable northern hemisphere areas for outdoor production include most of the northern Mediterranean countries, south-western England, along the relatively

*S. leucophylla clones,
from right to left:
'Stained Glass',
unnamed (from
Chipola), 'Bronze Urn',
'Schnell's Ghost',
unnamed, 'Persian
Carpet', 'Lipstick', 'Ruby
Tube', 'Crimson Snow'.
Although most of these
clones are typical for the
species, some show pos-
sible introgression (see
'History, habitat and
function'), which may
add to the commercial
desirability of these
striking plants.*

As in any new
industry, the pioneers
will reap the greatest
profits. Planning and
propagating for com-
mercial production
takes many years, and
this can be staged to
spread capitalisation
over many years.
But the time to start
is now, right at the
beginning of the third
millennium, while
there is no chance of
being beaten to the
early markets.

CUT PITCHERS

Pitchers are easy to handle as cut flowers,
and are perhaps one of the lowest mainte-
nance plants for this purpose. Their cutting
season (depending on the growth pattern of
the plants selected) extends from early
summer to early winter, with harvesting
usually needed only once a week. Only
about one pitcher in three should be harvested over the whole of the growing season, or the plants will be weakened and
produce noticeably smaller pitchers in the
next season.

Young pitchers two to three weeks old
are often too soft to be cut, and start to
shrivel within a few hours of picking. Older
pitchers are firmer, but for many varieties it
is hard to tell how mature they are because
there is little colour change as they age. For
this reason, the best commercial varieties
are those with self-indicating colour
changes, their pitchers usually becoming
more richly coloured over time. The age of
such pitchers can often be recognised at a
glance, though their mature colour may
vary somewhat over the season.

Cut pitchers must be kept moist and
cool until stood in water. They are often cut

warm western coast of Scotland to Ireland,
and over much of the USA. In the southern hemisphere, reversed seasons mean that
pitchers could be produced for 'off-season'
export to the much larger northern hemisphere markets, as well as for local sale.
Southern areas with an ideal climate for
commercial production include a considerable portion of non-tropical Australia,
much of New Zealand, South Africa and
many parts of southern South America.

S. x 'Firemouth' — tall
and upright with pitchers
maturing to red when
they are ready to cut.

about 15 centimetres (6 inches) from the bottom of the tube, leaving most dead insects and detritus below as a nutrient source for the plant. Taller pitchers can also be cut from the same plants, but may need to be gently hosed out to remove decaying insects (although odour is not usually noticeable unless hundreds of pitchers are grouped closely together).

Once in water, the life of the pitcher can be extended by reducing bacterial action. Some florists do this effectively and cheaply by adding a pinch of swimming-pool chlorine to around 10 litres (2.5 gallons) of water, but for home use even an aspirin will do a similar job.

The cutting season can be extended in many ways, most obviously by using appropriate varieties. For example in areas with light frosts only, White Pitcher will look good and can be cut as late as mid-winter. Many hybrids will produce pitchers over most of the growing season, though these aren't necessarily uniform in quality for all of that time. Pitchers can also be 'forced' into growth up to six weeks earlier by using a plastic cloche, or other light greenhouse material, but this should be removed before hot weather sets in.

Pitchers cut for sale don't have to be perfect — small blemishes or spots are usually inconspicuous on boldly patterned tubes, and don't affect their keeping properties. However, it is essential to check with purchasing florists as to what is required for their market.

∧ *A Sarracenia flower mix picked in midsummer.*

It is worth mentioning that *Sarracenia* flowers may also be saleable. Though fetching a lower price than the pitchers, they begin to appear weeks before saleable pitchers can be cut, and removing them saves the plants from wasting energy in seed formation. Unlike the pitchers, flowers should be cut the day they are opening, after which they will keep their petals for up to two weeks if kept cool.

SELECTING VARIETIES FOR SALE

Florists prefer tall and upright pitchers, but some are happy to take smaller quantities of more unusual varieties as well. Although taller pitchers will always sell at a premium price, don't let this put you off any really striking smaller clones — some of these grow so quickly and densely they can produce three or four times as many pitchers in the same area as a larger variety.

Selection of hybrids is perhaps the most critical part of setting up for commercial cut pitcher production. 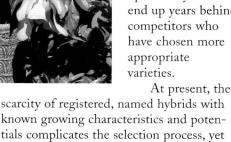 All hybrids selected for cutting should be faster growing than most species, and preferably grow over a longer season. If you take shortcuts and end up with slow-growing or unreliable varieties as the backbone of your operation you will end up years behind competitors who have chosen more appropriate varieties.

At present, the scarcity of registered, named hybrids with known growing characteristics and potentials complicates the selection process, yet many hundreds of excellent clones are already available worldwide. There is no need to decide which are the *very* best immediately — many hybrids look fairly alike, and the fastest-growing aren't necessarily much more vigorous than others which are equally saleable.

Once a cut pitcher industry is well established, there will be an ever-increasing number of new clones offered as competition for the older varieties. These will be registered, some even patented. All commercially desirable types will include performance figures which will likely be exaggerated in most cases.

But even a few decades after the cut pitcher industry establishes, its mainstay is likely to be the varieties that are available right now — and many of these will stand the test of time for decades longer. While newer varieties are still being tested and sometimes proven, it will be the best plants available *now* that will bring maximum returns over the first few decades of the 21st century. For this reason, any grower with a well-selected range of twenty to thirty attractive hybrids is likely to remain in business for a very long time, even without adding to the initial range.

Finding such varieties is not difficult. Look out for attractive and fast-growing hybrids and selected species forms grown by collectors in your area, and wherever you ultimately plan to grow them. They don't have to be named, and you don't need to name or register them unless you are hoping to sell them to other cut pitcher growers in later years. Indeed, quite a few of the named cultivars presently available grow relatively slowly, and have been selected for looks rather than vigour; these types may be less useful for cut pitchers than the diverse unnamed plants to be found.

Keep in mind that you will need years to multiply every really striking variety you find, whether using conventional division or tissue culture. Buy up all promising clones you can find, and keep them well labelled. This will be the least expensive part of your investment in both time and money. The best potential commercial clones grow very fast indeed, often so fast that growers who need to conserve space are happy to sell off large quantities cheaply, rather than just throw them away as they often have to do!

HOW BIG AN AREA FOR AN ADEQUATE RETURN?

There is no need to work on a huge scale to make a comfortable living from cut pitchers. An area of 0.4 hectare (one acre) can be set up by one person, usually with fewer problems than a larger area. Smaller production areas are also easier to manage, making it possible to use poison-free weed control methods such as fire or steam while the pitchers are dormant in winter.

Prices for pitchers depend mainly on size and colour, and different varieties should be kept separate when cut. The florists who buy them may choose to mix them, but growers should keep them grouped for maximum initial impact. They are visually most appealing when presented in small, single variety bunches, even of just three pitchers.

Reasonable estimates of potential returns based on present prices are given on page 97, although prices can be expected to reduce slightly with time as more growers enter the market. Running costs are small for established plantings because they need no fertiliser and, in small areas, no pesticides either, while herbicides would cause more damage to the pitchers than to competing weeds.

Supplying direct to selected florists can potentially gross 30–50 per cent more than the wholesale figures estimated later but requires an air-conditioned delivery van (with provision for keeping the pitchers moist at all times), and assumes that the

S. leucophylla x S. x areolata
— *delicately muted colours
and a flaring hood.*

growing site is reasonably close to a large city. All aspects of such a single-acre operation can still be handled by one person carrying out all processes from weed control to harvest and delivery, with the workload spread over a normal working week of one to two days harvesting and packing, and one day spent on deliveries.

BUILDING UP IN STAGES

Setting up for commercial production is a long-term process. It is likely to take as long as ten or twelve years unless you are willing to invest massively in very large quantities of suitable commercial varieties — assuming these are available! This is not necessarily a disadvantage, as overly ambitious growers are more likely to make mistakes in their initial choices of 'best' varieties than people who take the time to adequately assess a smaller range.

Careful planning and staging can allow you to start an entire operation in your backyard, even before you have bought suitable land. The most significant costs associated with setting up a commercial pitcher operation are land, peaty soil, and a reliable water supply, in that order. The obvious stages are:

COLLECTING AND PLANNING Test a variety of clones that grow best in your area as well as a variety of other promising clones for which little or no information is available. Unless you already have access to excep-

tional clones, it is best to start by contacting collectors and trialling the best of the varieties you can source from them. It may also be worth collecting unusual clones that may be useful for breeding new varieties later.

BUILDING UP STOCKS You should build up large stocks of the most promising varieties from your trials. Avoid using plants which are already named or patented — these are aimed mainly at collectors and are usually expensive. There are hundreds or perhaps even thousands of better clones for cut pitcher production worldwide.

SELECT SUITABLE LAND The ideal land will have adequate and suitable water supplies (discussed below). The growing soil will almost certainly need to be made peatier, and this is also discussed separately.

START SMALL Plant out on a small scale at first, splitting and dividing the best clones (of which you should have a good range by now) every year or two. Some may grow relatively poorly once they are planted out, but this will not be a problem if you have tested a diverse range of attractive forms, and the rest are growing well.

BE PATIENT Don't start harvesting until plants are close to their mature size. A few pitchers can be cut for market

< S. x 'Ritter's Pet' — a tall variety of unknown ancestry, with a handsome shape which more than compensates for subdued colour.

> S. x 'Big Red' (S. purpurea x [S. flava x S. rubra]).

< S. x 'Flair' (S. flava x [S. rubra x S. purpurea]) x S. leu-cophylla. *A smaller growing White Pitcher look-alike which produces many more pitchers over a longer season.*

> S. x 'Night Sky' (S. rubra subsp. gulfensis x S. leucophylla) — *a smaller upright variety with exceptional colour contrast.*

S. x exornata (S. alata x
S. purpurea subsp.
venosa) — not a
cut-flower type as the
pitchers remain soft,
but with obvious
prospects for further
breeding.

testing (either by your wholesaler or your-self) from about two years before this stage. Don't dispose of varieties which aren't sell-ing well initially — remember that these spectacular plants are still unfamiliar in many places. Once spectacular and unequivocally beautiful clones such as the diverse forms of White Pitcher are recog-nised and sought on the market, all other good varieties will also be in demand with-in a short time.

CHOOSING A SITE

The most important criterion when choos-ing a site suitable for commercial culture is a reliable supply of relatively soft water that will hold out even through a prolonged drought. In some places summer rainfall will be adequate, but a reserve supply from a dam or pond is essential as even two dry weeks may be enough to depress pitcher production.

The softest water generally runs off fairly steep slopes, where it doesn't have time to pick up much in the way of dis-solved salts. On the other hand, slopes are expensive to turn into boggy terraces as earthmoving costs increase exponentially with slope angle.

A fairly level site at the base of a slope is ideal, though if too steep the slope will cast too much shade for good production. Both soil and water need enough sun to warm them through the growing season, while the pitchers colour best with abun-dant sunlight. However, excessively strong sunlight can be a disadvantage in areas with a hot, dry summer, in which case 50 per cent shadecloth over all of the growing area may be needed.

All of these and other related issues were discussed earlier (see Chapter 3) but are mentioned again because the more closely a site matches natural *Sarracenia* environments, the less will be needed in the way of potentially expensive modifications or shading.

SOILS

Preparing suitable soils for *Sarracenia* is probably the second most difficult problem for cut pitcher production after identifying the best available clones. These plants need peaty soils, and peat is formed from plant matter which breaks down slowly underwater. So-called substitutes such as coco-peat decay rapidly when kept wet.

It is unlikely that most cheap peat substitutes will work any better once exposed to air — peat forms in the relative absence of oxygen, and is really just undecayed

S. x exornata x S. leucophylla *bred from a variant of the previous plant illustrated.*

plant remnants. Substitutes for wild-collected peat such as waterlogged straw can be mixed with sandy soils to create an underlying water reservoir from 10–15 centimetres (4–6 inches) below the peat substrate. However, these take too long to break down to make adequate soil for the upper layer. Some forms of soft brown coal (lignite) are effectively fossilised peat, and can be milled to make a good replacement, but these vary considerably in quality so test them on a small scale first.

Peat mining is a well-publicised environmental issue, although it can be harvested sustainably. Irish peat bogs have been harvested for fuel on a massive scale for perhaps millennia, yet in parts of that small country the peat continues to accumulate as fast as it is removed. In Canada, another very cold and poorly drained country but with far more massive reserves of peat, the harvest only skims the surface of what is available. In the Southern Hemisphere,

New Zealand peat is only exploited in a limited way. So why the drama?

There is actually a good reason to worry about peat habitats in the United Kingdom, because this is a relatively small, cold, and heavily populated country. Peat bogs here are a significant habitat for many plants which are found nowhere else, so harvesting peat is a problem because it displaces or destroys many of these plant species.

In the United Kingdom most peat is used for the 'traditional' John Innes potting mixes rather than specialised peat-bog plants. These are perhaps the most water-repellent soil mixes in the world if you allow them to dry out even once — and I have tested quite a few. Their hydrophobic properties are largely due to the use of peat in the mix. Many nurseries worldwide now avoid using peat in any mixes (except for peat-requiring plants), not only for environmental reasons, but also because of the

S. x 'Alien Banana'
(S. psittacina x S. alata)
— the rich colour and
prolific pitcher
production make this a
potential commercial
variety despite its
unusual shape.

problems in getting them to absorb water.

If peat wasn't being used for such mixes, peat harvesting for horticulture could easily be reduced to sustainable levels even within the United Kingdom. Certainly, the potential cut *Sarracenia* pitcher industry could be provided with all the peat it needs in its entirety without slowing down the rate of new peat deposition worldwide by any appreciable degree.

Around 25 square kilometres (10 square miles) of cut pitcher plantations should produce around a billion pitchers per year, perhaps much more if planted with selected varieties. Assuming this to be the level at which cut pitcher plantings stabilise, let us consider how much peat this uses.

With about 50 per cent peat worked 15 centimetres (6 inches) deep into fairly sandy soils, the peat requirement for establishing these 25 square kilometres is likely to be less than two million cubic metres. The whole of this amount can be harvested from less than a square kilometre of peat bog. Some top dressing would also be required perhaps once a decade, using around 20 per cent of the original amount each time, only a fiftieth of the original amount of peat required.

Worldwide, new peat is being formed at vastly greater rates than this.

Environmentally, there is nothing wrong with harvesting peat — the problem is one of over-harvesting it for unnecessary purposes.

TISSUE CULTURE

The propagation of desirable *Sarracenia* clones can be a slow process, and many nurseries specialising in these plants have taken to tissue culture for speeding up the production of larger numbers of saleable plants. This method raises sterile plantlets in a nutrient-enriched gel until they are ready to plant out into a soil mix. It is cost-ly because tiny, sterile propagules can only be prepared in specially set up laboratories, by people experienced in such work.

The major advantage of tissue culture is that it produces a great number of genetically identical plants in a relatively short time, but these are very small and in many plant groups may grow abnormally to begin with. In the case of *Sarracenia*, plantlets cultured in this way tend to produce multiple growing tips, criss-crossing each other and forming a tangle of stunted pitchers. This problem can be overcome by dividing them up regularly for three or four years, but you will end up with numerous small plants after this time, all of them years away from producing pitchers large enough to cut.

Seeds raised by tissue culture methods are less prone to producing multiple heads and can therefore produce cut pitchers in less time. However, the somewhat variable pitchers of seedling hybrid plants may not be acceptable to wholesalers, who usually demand a degree of uniformity. Also, the faster that seed is raised under optimally controlled conditions, the more difficult the resulting plants are to adapt to growth outdoors. Many may die in the transition, and it is likely that these are the plants which would have been selected out much earlier under more natural growth conditions.

More significantly for the cut pitcher industry, tissue culture could become a way of shipping highly selected commercial clones internationally. The tubes of such plants will almost invariably be hybrids, and so will not be affected by conservation laws designed to protect the species. More importantly, the plants inside each clear, sealed tube can be guaranteed to be free of disease or fungal problems, because if the culture wasn't sterile to start with it would already have failed.

Conventional propagation methods will produce saleable cut pitchers much faster than will tissue culture, always in

∧ S. x 'Fledgling' (S. x wrigleyana x S. leucophylla). Although three-quarters White Pitcher, this hybrid is unusually shaped.

∨ S. x excellens, diverse unnamed clones, with a single pitcher of S. alata 'Red Mouth' x S. minor at right.

larger quantities right from the start, and much less expensively. However, tissue culture will have its place in the developing industry. In part, it will be a way of producing relatively disease-free plants from choice clones which have had their productivity depressed by low-grade viral infections. But most importantly, it will be a way of spreading the best and most vigorous clones between countries, with minimal quarantine problems.

LIVING WITH WILD PLANTS

Ironically, a cultivated cut pitcher industry would face its greatest establishment problems in the USA, because it could potentially interfere with conservation of the remaining wild populations. Although present laws protecting wild plants are still generally weak, this will change with time as understanding of the increasingly desperate need for conservation grows. For this reason commercial sites should be chosen well away from remaining wild populations so there is no chance of hybrid pollen contaminating wild stands — or of having the plantation destroyed later because of the potential for genetic contamination of precious wild stands!

Almost as important for growers in the USA is planting only hybrid plants, or registered clones of species. It is likely that the wild harvest of cut pitchers will become illegal with time, even though commercial exploitation has probably saved some populations from complete destruction for the moment. Ultimately, growers may need to be able to prove that they sell only named and formally registered clones or hybrids. This will also help to prevent 'laundering' of pitchers poached from the wild and sold as if they were from cultivated plants.

The cut pitcher industry has the potential to be regarded as the ultimate in environmentally sound business practice. It should draw minimally and sustainably on wild resources, using no synthetic fertilisers or poisonous sprays, and the cut pitchers won't affect the health of asthmatics or other chemically sensitive people as many sprayed cut flowers do.

And it will be pleasing if right from the beginning growers weren't just thinking about profits, but had also looked to the preservation of the wild plants from which their industry was born, and upon which it will depend for long-term renewal.

RETURN ESTIMATES FOR CUT PITCHER PRODUCTION

All figures below are based on prices prevailing in the year 2000.

UNITED STATES OF AMERICA The present USA market is dominated by wild-harvested White Pitchers, but this will change as an increasingly diverse range of hybrid pitchers becomes available, and legislation increasingly constrains the use of natural populations. Using the same conservative figures (for White Pitcher only) as above, and an approximate return of US$1.00 per good quality pitcher (less commission if sold through a wholesaler), a return of over US$100 000 per hectare per year (US$40 000 per acre) could reasonably be expected. This may be much higher later if protective legislation for remaining wild stands is introduced before the first harvests of cultivated plants begin.

AUSTRALIA Good-quality pitchers (sold within Australia) presently wholesale at around AU$1.50, while smaller varieties are about half this price. Tall pitchers of *S. leucophylla* bring the best prices at present, mainly because seed of this species is readily available in large quantities, and because the plants are relatively uniform (despite some natural variation) as well as spectacular. However, this fairly slow-growing plant can only be harvested at around 20 to 30 pitchers per square metre over a growing season, and it is also restricted to two main pitcher-production seasons in late spring and early autumn, with the best coloured pitchers appearing in autumn.

Using the more conservative figures above, an acre (0.4 hectare) planted with this species will yield at least 60 000 pitchers per year (allowing for the area taken up by walking paths of boards between the plants to minimise soil compaction). This represents a potential income (after wholesale commission is deducted — generally around 25–30 per cent) of at least AU$150 000 per hectare ($60 000 per acre).

Using equivalently-sized and brilliantly coloured hybrids, the yield of pitchers can be as much as doubled for some of the best growers. Smaller hybrids with intense colour such as the dwarf *S. leucophylla* look-alike 'Flair', can produce yields of three times as many pitchers. Even at AU$0.75 for these smaller pitchers, this is still a 50 per cent increase over the taller but less productive White Pitcher.

WORLDWIDE CONTACTS

The list below (courtesy of Gordon Ohlenrott) was correct at the end of the year 2000. Specialist carnivorous plant societies that don't deal with *Sarracenia* have not been included.

UNITED STATES OF AMERICA

Bay Area Carnivorous Plant Society
39011 Applegate Terrace
Fremont
California CA 94536

International Carnivorous Plant Society
(*The* central international source of carnivorous plant information)
The Fullerton Arboretum
California State University
Fullerton CA 92634
www.carnivorousplants.org

Los Angeles Carnivorous Plant Society
PO Box 12281
Glendale CA 91224 - 0981

Tampa Bay Carnivorous Plant Club
4202 E. Fowler Avenue USF 3108
Tampa, FL 33620

AUSTRALIA

Australian Carnivorous Plant Society
PO Box 391
St Agnes, South Australia, 5097

Carnivorous Plant Society of New South Wales
PO Box 87
Burwood, NSW, 2134

Victorian Carnivorous Plant Society
PO Box 201
South Yarra, Victoria, 3141

CANADA

Pacific North West Carnivorous Plant Club
c/o Laurence Ho
PO Box 42008
South Oak
Vancouver BC
V5N 4J6

CZECH REPUBLIC

Darwiniana
Zdenek Zacek
Ustavni 139
Praha 8
181 00

FRANCE

M. Gerard Lecointe
Dionée Association Francaise d'Amateurs de Plantes Carnivores
8 Rue de Boufflers
78100 St Germain-En-Laye

GERMANY

Gesellschaft für Fleischfressende Pflanzen
Frank Gallep
Zweibrückenstrasse 31
D 40625, Düsseldorf

ISRAEL

Carnivorous Plant Society of Israel
c/o Dr Daniel M. Joel
Department of Weed Research
Newe-Ya'ar Research Centre
Newe-Ya'ar
Haifa 31900

ITALY

Italian Carnivorous Plant Society
Marcello Catalano
Via Ronchi 2
20134 Milano

JAPAN

Insectivorous Plant Society
Department of Biology
Nippon Dental University
Fujimi — Chiyoda-ku
Tokyo 102

Japan Carnivorous Plant Society
Naoke Tanabe
1-4-6 Minami Hanazono
Hanamigawa-ku
Chiba City
Chiba Pref.
262-0022

UNITED KINGDOM

Edinburgh Carnivorous Plant Society
c/o Mrs J. Whyte
'Lingardswood'
Viewfield Road
Nr. West Calder EH5 8XF
Scotland

The Carnivorous Plant Society
c/o Malcolm Goddard
94 Uplands Road, Woodford Bridge
Essex IG8 8JW

BIBLIOGRAPHY

The references below include all primary written sources for this book, but are not intended to be a complete bibliography of the genus. Article titles have been shortened in some cases, and journal names are cited in full for the benefit of readers not familiar with their abbreviations.

J & J Ainsworth, 1996. *Sarracenia: North American Pitcher Plants*. Woking, Surrey: National Council for the Conservation of Plants and Gardens.

AS Baldwin, 2000. A record of desiccated rotifers in a single trap of the Yellow pitcher plant *Sarracenia flava* with notes on their distribution and rehydration rates, *Journal of the Elisha Mitchell Scientific Society* 116: 69.

NG Barker & GB Williamson, 1988. Effects of a winter fire on *Sarracenia alata* and *S. psittacina*, *American Journal of Botany* 75(1): 138–143.

RJ Bayer, L Hufford & DE Soltis, 1996. Phylogenetic relationships in Sarraceniaceae based on rbcL and ITS sequences, *Systematic Botany* 21(2): 121–134.

CR Bell, 1952. Natural hybrids of the genus *Sarracenia*, *Journal of the Elisha Mitchell Scientific Society* 68: 55–80.

CR Bell & FW Case, 1956. Natural hybrids in the genus *Sarracenia* II, *Journal of the Elisha Mitchell Scientific Society* 72: 142–152.

S Benjamin & R Sutter, 1993. *Sarracenia jonesii* Wherry (Mountain sweet pitcher plant), *Natural Areas Journal* 13(2): 124–129.

LA Bledski & AM Ellison, 1998. Population growth and production of *Habrotrocha rosa* (Rotifera) and its contribution to the nutrient supply of its host, the northern pitcher plant *Sarracenia purpurea*, *Hydrobiologia* 385: 193–200.

L Borgen, W Greuter, DL Hawksworth, DH Nicolson & B Zimmer, 1998. Announcing a test and trial phase for the registration of new plant names (1998–1999), *Carnivorous Plant Newsletter* 27(1): 25–26.

J Boulay, 1995. Carnivorous plants, micropropagation assays [in French], *Bulletin des Académie et Société Lorraines des Sciences* 34(3): 151–159.

WE Bradshaw, PA Armbruster & CM Holzapfel, 1998. Fitness consequences of hibernal diapause in the pitcher plant mosquito, *Wyeomyia smithii*, *Ecology* 79(4): 1458–1462.

WE Bradshaw & LP Lounibos, 1977. Evolution of dormancy and its photoperiodic control in pitcher-plant mosquitoes, *Evolution* 31(3): 546–567.

JS Brewer, 1999. Short-term effects of fire and competition and plasticity of the Yellow pitcher plant *Sarracenia alata*, *American Journal of Botany* 86: 1264–1271.

R Brummitt, 1999. Report of the Committee for Spermatophyta, *Taxon* 48: 359–371.

CJ Cameron, GL Donald & CG Paterson, 1977. Oxygen–fauna relationships in the pitcher plant *Sarracenia purpurea* with reference to the chironomid *Metriocnemus knabi*, *Canadian Journal of Zoology* 55(12): 2018–2023.

FW Case, 1992. Carnivorous plants for bog gardens, *Bulletin of the American Rock Garden Society* 50(3): 205–210.

FW Case & RB Case, 1974. *Sarracenia alabamensis*, a newly recognised species from central Alabama, *Rhodora* 76: 650–665.

CT Chapin & J Pastor, 1995. Nutrient limitations in the northern pitcher plant *Sarracenia purpurea*, *Canadian Journal of Botany* 73(5): 728–734.

M Cheek, 1988. *Sarracenia psittacina*, *Kew Magazine* 5: 60–65.

M Cheek, D Schnell, JL Reveal & J

Schlauer, 1997. Proposal to conserve the name *Sarracenia purpurea* (Sarraceniaceae) with a new type, *Taxon* 46(4): 781–783.

M Cheek & M Yough, 1994. The *Limonium peregrinum* of Carolus Clusius in *Carnivorous Plant Newsletter* 23(4): 95–98.

NL Christensen, 1976. The role of carnivory in *Sarracenia flava* with regard to specific nutrient deficiencies, *Journal of the Elisha Mitchell Scientific Society* 92(4): 144–147.

S Clemesha, 1979. *Sarracenia* species, Australia in *Carnivorous Plant Newsletter* 8(4): 106–108.

S Clemesha, 1987. *Sarracenia* — the hairy ones, *Carnivorous Plant Newsletter* 16(2): 49–53.

DL Cochran-Stafira & CN von Ende, 1998. Integrating bacteria into food webs: studies with *Sarracenia purpurea* inquilines, *Ecology* 79(3): 880–898.

P D'Amato, 1998. *The Savage Garden.* Berkeley, California; Ten Speed Press.

CD Darlington & AP Wylie, 1961. *Chromosome Atlas of Flowering Plants.* London; George Allen and Unwin.

LE Debuhr, 1977. Wood anatomy of the Sarraceniaceae; ecological and evolutionary implications, *Plant Systematics and Evolution* 128(3/4): 159–170.

R Determann, 1993. A new cultivar of *Sarracenia leucophylla, Carnivorous Plant Newsletter* 22(4): 107–108.

WJ Dress, SJ Newell, AJ Nastase & JC Ford, 1997. Analysis of amino acids in nectar from pitchers of *Sarracenia purpurea, American Journal of Botany* 84(12): 1701–1706.

D Fish, 1976. Insect–plant relationships of the insectivorous pitcher plant *Sarracenia minor, Florida Entomology* 59(2): 199–203.

D Fish & DW Hall, 1978. Succession and stratification of aquatic insects inhabiting the leaves of the insectivorous pitcher plant *Sarracenia purpurea, American Midland Naturalist* 99(1): 172–183.

DR Folkerts & GW Folkerts, 1996. Aids for field identification of pitcher plant moths of the genus *Exyra, Entomological News* 107(3): 128–136.

GW Folkerts, 1990. Facultative rhizome dimorphism in *Sarracenia psittacina*, an adaptation to deepening substrate, *Phytomorphology* 39(4): 285–290.

GW Folkerts & DR Folkerts, 1989. Unique capsule dehiscence in *Sarracenia leucophylla* and a hypothesis concerning post-anthesis tilting in *Sarracenia* flowers, *Castanea* 54(2): 111–114.

DR Gallie & Chang Su-Chih, 1997. Signal transduction in the carnivorous plant *Sarracenia purpurea*. Regulation of secretory hydrolase expression during development and in response to resources, *Plant Physiology* 115(4): 1461–1471.

R Gibson, 1993. The *Sarracenia rubra* complex, *Bulletin of the Australian Carnivorous Plant Society* 12(2): 11–16.

R Gibson, 1998. A few weeks in a carnivorous plant paradise, *Bulletin of the Australian Carnivorous Plant Society* 17(3): 3–7.

MJW Godt & JL Hamrick, 1996. Genetic structure of two endangered pitcher plants, *S. jonesii* and *S. oreophila, American Journal of Botany* 83(8): 1016–1023.

MJW Godt & JL Hamrick, 1999. Genetic divergence among infraspecific taxa of *Sarracenia purpurea, Systematic Botany* 23: 427–438.

M Groves, 1998. Atlanta Botanical Garden, *The Carnivorous Plant Society Journal* 21: 9–12.

M Groves, 1998. Atlanta Botanical Garden Conservation Program, *The Carnivorous Plant Society Journal* 21: 13–17.

RV Hamilton, RL Petersen & RM Duffield, 1998. An unusual occurrence of caddisfly in a Pennsylvania population of the purple pitcher plant *Sarracenia purpurea, Entomological News* 109(1): 36.

RV Hamilton, M Whitaker, TC Farmer, AA Benn & RM Duffield, 1996. A report of *Chaulioides* (Megaloptera: Corydalidae) in the purple pitcher plant *Sarracenia purpurea, Journal of the Kansas Entomological Society* 69(3): 257–259.

T Hannam, 1994. *Sarracenia* in the Far North [of Australia], *Bulletin of the Australian Carnivorous Plant Society* 13(1): 11.

B Hanrahan & B Meyers-Rice, 2000. New *Sarracenia* cultivars – 'Adrian Slack', *Carnivorous Plant Newsletter* 29(4): 116–117.

E Harvey & TE Miller, 1996. Variance in composition of inquiline communities in leaves of *Sarracenia purpurea* on multiple spatial scales, *Oecologia* 108(3): 562–566.

SB Heard, 1994. Pitcher plant midges and mosquitoes: a processing chain at work, *Ecology* 75(1): 647–660.

SB Heard, 1998. Capture rates of invertebrate prey by the pitcher plant *Sarracenia purpurea, American Midland Naturalist* 139(1): 79–89.

K Jaffe, F Michelangeli, JM Gonzalez, B Miras & MC Ruiz, 1992. Carnivory in pitcher plants of the genus *Heliamphora* (Sarraceniaceae), *New Phytologist* 122: 733–744.

DM Joel, 1989. Mimicry in carnivorous pitcher plants — fact or legend? *Carnivorous Plant Newsletter* 18(1): 12–14.

BS John, 1979. *The World of Ice: The Natural History of the Frozen Regions.* London; Orbis Publishing.

D Kutt, 1977. *Sarracenia* — Tour Deluxe, *Carnivorous Plant Newsletter* 6(1): 35–37.

L Kyte, 1987. *Plants from Test Tubes.* Portland, Oregon; Timber Press.

R Lamb, 1989. *Sarracenia purpurea* in western Canada, *Carnivorous Plant Newsletter* 18(1): 7–8.

S Locke, 1998. *Sarracenia* in the Apalachicola National Forest, northern Florida, *The Carnivorous Plant Society Journal* 21: 49–56.

A Lowrie, 1997. Experiences in breaking dormancy in carnivorous plant seed, *The Carnivorous Plant Society Journal* 20: 24–32.

S McDaniel, 1971. The genus *Sarracenia, Bulletin of the Tall Timbers Research Station* 9: 1–36.

AJ Mandossian, 1966. Germination of seeds in *Sarracenia purpurea, Michigan Botanist* 5: 67–79.

AD Marmelstein, 1973. Field observations on *Sarracenia, Carnivorous Plant Newsletter* 2(1): 5–6.

L Mellichamp, 1987. New cultivars of *Sarracenia, Carnivorous Plant Newsletter* 16(2): 39–42.

L Mellichamp, 1992. Hybrid pitcher plants, *Bulletin of the American Rock Garden Society* 50(1): 3–10.

L Mellichamp & R Gardner, 1998. New cultivars of *Sarracenia* from North Carolina: 'Dixie Lace' and 'Ladies-in-Waiting', *Carnivorous Plant Newsletter* 27(2): 38–40.

B Meyers-Rice, 1993. Arkham Pond: profile of a South Carolina Wetland, *Bulletin of the Australian Carnivorous Plant Society* 12(4): 4–6.

B Meyers-Rice, 2001. Black Vine Weevil: a *Sarracenia* and *Darlingtonia* pest, *Carnivorous Plant Newsletter* 30(1): 26–27

B Meyers-Rice, 2001. Rare *Sarracenia* Poaching and the ICPS, *Carnivorous Plant Newsletter* 30(2):43–50.

J Miller, 1980. The Green Swamp and Atlantic Coast trip, *Carnivorous Plant Newsletter* 9(3/4): 66–68/95–97.

PB Murphy & RS Boyd, 1999. Population status and habitat characterisation of the endangered *Sarracenia rubra* subspecies *alabamensis*, *Castanea* 64: 101–113.

RFC Naczi, EM Soper, FW Case & RB Case, 1999. *Sarracenia rosea*, a new species of pitcher plant from the southeastern United States, *Sida* 18(4): 1183–1206.

EC Nelson. 1999. A carnivorous plant on an Irish Postage Stamp: David Moore and *Sarracenia* hybrids at Glasnevin Botanic Gardens, *Carnivorous Plant Newsletter* 28(1): 3–7.

SJ Newell & AJ Nastase, 1998. Efficiency of insect capture by *Sarracenia purpurea*, the northern pitcher plant, *American Journal of Botany* 85(1): 88–91.

G Ohlenrott, 1996. *Carnivorous Plants: Total Listing*. Melbourne, Australia; Victorian Carnivorous Plant Society.

FK Parrish & EJ Rykiel, 1979. Okefenokee Swamp origin: review and reconsideration, *Journal of the Elisha Mitchell Scientific Society* 95: 17–31.

RL Petersen, L Hanley, E Walsh, H Hunt & RM Duffield, 1997. Occurrence of the rotifer *Habrotrocha* cf. *rosa*, the purple pitcher plant *Sarracenia purpurea* along the eastern seaboard of North America, *Hydrobiologia* 354 (September): 63–66.

B Pierson, 1985. *Sarracenia* in the rain, *Bulletin of the Australian Carnivorous Plant Society* 4(3): 74.

B Pierson, 1989. Collection and storage of *Sarracenia* pollen, *Bulletin of the Australian Carnivorous Plant Society* 8(4): 70–71.

AB Prankevicius & DM Cameron, 1990. Free-living dinitrogen fixing bacteria in the leaf of the northern pitcher plant *Sarracenia purpurea*, *Naturaliste Canadien* 116(4): 245–250.

I Rojo-Herguedas & JL Olmo, 1999. The ciliated protozoa of the pitcher plant *Sarracenia purpurea*, *Acta Protozoologica* 38(2): 155.

N Romanowski, 1998. *Planting Wetlands and Dams: A Practical Guide to Wetland Design, Construction and Propagation*. Sydney; UNSW Press.

N Romanowski, 2000. *Water Garden Plants and Animals: The Complete Guide for All Australia*. Sydney; UNSW Press.

J Schlauer. 1998. The correct naming of carnivorous plants: ICBN, ICNC, and the roles of CPN and ICPS, *Carnivorous Plant Newsletter* 27(1): 27–28.

DE Schnell, 1974. *Sarracenia* — destructive insect associates: a summary, *Carnivorous Plant Newsletter* 3(3): 35–37.

DE Schnell, 1976. *Carnivorous Plants of the United States and Canada*. North Carolina; John F. Blair.

DE Schnell, 1977. Infraspecific variation in *Sarracenia rubra*: some observations, *Castanea* 42(2): 149–170.

DE Schnell, 1978a. *Sarracenia* petal extract chromatography, *Castanea* 43(2): 107–115.

DE Schnell, 1978b. Systematic flower studies in *Sarracenia*, *Castanea* 43(4): 211–220.

DE Schnell, 1979. A critical review of published variants of *Sarracenia purpurea*, *Castanea* 44(1): 47–59.

DE Schnell, 1980. Notes on the biology of *Sarracenia oreophila*, *Castanea* 45(2): 166–170.

D[E] Schnell, 1989. *Sarracenia alata* and *S. leucophylla* variations, *Carnivorous Plant Newsletter* 18(3): 79–83.

DE Schnell, 1993. *Sarracenia purpurea* subspecies *venosa* variety *burkii* of the Gulf coastal plain, *Rhodora* 95: 6–10.

D[E] Schnell, 1994. Cattle as *Sarracenia* stewards? *Carnivorous Plant Newsletter* 23(2): 49–52.

D[E] Schnell, 1998a. *Sarracenia flava* varieties, *Carnivorous Plant Newsletter*

27(4): 116–120.

DE Schnell, 1998b. A pitcher key to the genus *Sarracenia*, *Castanea* 63(4): 489–492.

DE Schnell & RO Determann, 1997. *Sarracenia purpurea* subspecies *venosa* variety *montana*: a new variety, *Castanea* 62(1): 60–62.

KE Schwaegerle & BA Schaal, 1979. Genetic variability and founder effect in the pitcher plant *Sarracenia purpurea*, *Evolution* 33(4): 1210–1218.

P Sheridan, 1996. Noteworthy *Sarracenia* collections II, *Carnivorous Plant Newsletter* 25(1): 19–23.

P Sheridan, 1996. The hooded pitcher plant *Sarracenia minor* at its southern limit, *Carnivorous Plant Newsletter* 25(2): 39–41.

PM Sheridan & RR Mills, 1998. Presence of pro-anthocyanidins in mutant green *Sarracenia* indicate blockage in later anthocyanin biosynthesis between leucocyanidin and pseudobase, *Plant Science* 135(1): 11–16.

P Sheridan & B Scholl, 1993. *Sarracenia purpurea* ssp. *purpurea* f. *heterophylla* in Nova Scotia, *Carnivorous Plant Newsletter* 22(4): 106–107.

RB Simpson, 1994. *Kew Conservation Review: Pitchers in Trade*. Kew: Royal Botanic Gardens.

A Slack, 1981. *Carnivorous Plants*. London; Ebury Press.

A Slack, 1986. *Insect Eating Plants and How to Grow Them*. Dorset, England; Alphabooks.

B Tribe & P Wilson, 1998. Distinguishing between *Sarracenia oreophila* and *S. flava*, *The Carnivorous Plant Society Journal* 21: 57–61.

S Vogel, 1998. Remarkable nectaries: structure, ecology, organophyletic perspectives II, *Flora* 193(1): 1–29.

P Wilson, 1993. *Sarracenia rubra* subspecies forms, *Bulletin of the Australian Carnivorous Plant Society* 12(3): 11–13.

P Wilson, 1997. Heterophylla or green mutant *Sarracenia* forms, *The Carnivorous Plant Society Journal* 20: 33–39.

INDEX